Complicit

Complicit

HOW OUR CULTURE ENABLES
MISBEHAVING MEN

Reah Bravo

G

GALLERY BOOKS

NEW YORK LONDON TORONTO SYDNEY NEW DELHI

G

Gallery Books
An Imprint of Simon & Schuster, LLC
1230 Avenue of the Americas
New York, NY 10020

First Gallery Books hardcover edition June 2024

GALLERY BOOKS and colophon are registered trademarks of
Simon & Schuster, LLC

Some names and identifying details have been changed.

Simon & Schuster: Celebrating 100 Years of Publishing in 2024

For information about special discounts for bulk purchases,
please contact Simon & Schuster Special Sales at 1-866-506-1949 or
business@simonandschuster.com.

The Simon & Schuster Speakers Bureau can bring authors to
your live event. For more information or to book an event,
contact the Simon & Schuster Speakers Bureau at 1-866-248-3049
or visit our website at www.simonspeakers.com.

Interior design by Alexis Minieri

Manufactured in the United States of America

1   3   5   7   9   10   8   6   4   2

Library of Congress Cataloging-in-Publication Data

Names: Bravo, Reah, author.
Title: Complicit: how our culture enables misbehaving men / Reah Bravo.
Description: New York, NY : Gallery Books, [2024] | Includes
bibliographical references and index.
Identifiers: LCCN 2023043208 (print) | LCCN 2023043209 (ebook) |
ISBN 9781982154745 (hardcover) | ISBN 9781982154769 (ebook)
Subjects: LCSH: Sexual harassment. | Sex crimes. | Abused women.
Classification: LCC HF5549.5.S45 B75 2024 (print) | LCC HF5549.5.S45
(ebook) | DDC 331.4/133—dc23/eng/20240214
LC record available at https://lccn.loc.gov/2023043208
LC ebook record available at https://lccn.loc.gov/2023043209

ISBN 978-1-9821-5474-5
ISBN 978-1-9821-5476-9 (ebook)

For Saysay and Asa

Contents

Complicit

Introduction

Enough time has passed that I can say I regret calling Charlie Rose a sexual predator. This was in the *Washington Post*, back in November 2017, when I went on the record with accusations of sexual misconduct: "He was a sexual predator, and I was his victim." The story, in which seven other women said he had also made unwanted advances toward them, ended his term as a celebrated cultural icon. Charlie is now known as much for behavior that includes groping women and emerging unexpectedly naked in their presence as he is for his award-winning contributions to broadcast journalism.

I had endeavored to be as cautious as possible with what I told reporters, understanding the potential consequences of every one of my words, and the label "sexual predator" felt more than apt. Charlie, after all, was a powerful man who methodically singled out and targeted vulnerable women, using work as a pretense to isolate them in his home, his hotel rooms, and the cabins of his private flights. But as I spoke my truth, I hadn't stopped to consider that "sexual predator" is also a legal term that in some jurisdictions indicates a prior conviction for a criminal offense. Charlie didn't have any such criminal record.

This made "sexual predator" a word choice that played into the narratives being used by #MeToo's detractors, some of whom said the movement was recklessly lacking in nuance and due process. They said that accusers were failing to make distinctions between a pushy date and rape; between something creepy but technically within the bounds of the law and a heinous act of sexual violence; between one late-night lapse of drunken judgment and a habitual, systematic abuse of one's power. The critics held tightly to their sliding scale of bad behavior because it was comforting, because categories give us all a sense of clarity—legally and morally—along with an assurance of our own relative goodness.

What was actually far more difficult to comprehend than the variety of the injustice emerging from #MeToo was its sheer ubiquity. What did the pervasiveness of all this cruelty and mistreatment mean about the world in which we lived and worked? And what had this world demanded of each of us? Did we even have the language to say? So many of our lived experiences with sexism and misogyny didn't fit tidily into our established narratives about victimhood and abuse. For some of us, this helped make #MeToo go down like a mug of ayahuasca: a bitter, mind-altering, and sometimes nauseating journey back to experiences we thought we had understood but that we had never fully seen or processed. Yes, Charlie was indeed a kind of predator, and I had been his prey, but I was starting to see an ecosystem that we had both done our part to sustain.

When the *Post*'s investigative journalist Amy Brittain reached out to me, introducing herself and asking if I might be willing to chat about my experience working for Charlie, I had already begun to queasily revisit my time at his namesake on PBS. This was back in

2007 and 2008, first as an unpaid intern for one year and then as a producer for six months. His advances began early in my internship, and I had always struggled to understand why I stayed and fought so hard to get hired for a job that I knew would be absolute misery. Careerism was certainly a part of it, the fact that having *Charlie Rose* on my résumé would open doors—which it did. Another part of it was financial. I was a graduate student living off student loans and credit cards, and, amid a recession, the internship became my only foot in the door to salaried employment. So I doubled down. Three months before the global financial crisis, I graduated with a job in hand. Not all my classmates were as fortunate.

The details that I eventually provided Brittain were remarkably similar to accounts from other women, with the commonalities helping to cement our credibility. The reporting was ironclad, the victims were heard, and a powerful man was held accountable. More stories would follow in both the *Post* and other outlets, expanding the details and scope of Charlie's misconduct. And yet I found all of it—everything that had been exposed—disconcertingly inadequate. There had been a perversity and madness to working for Charlie that went well beyond his fame and institutional power. It also went beyond my youth, career aspirations, and need to pay rent. In fact, the most unsettling aspects of my encounters with Charlie didn't appear in any of the news stories—and more unnerving still was how much I struggled to name them myself. They remained elusive.

Joan Didion famously said, "I write entirely to find out what I'm thinking." With a similar compulsion, I began writing to find out what I *had been* thinking. I wanted to know why, instead of immediately putting a forceful end to Charlie's inappropriateness, I exhausted myself with pleasantries and attentive smiles. Why did I answer his lewd phone calls, silently endure his groping, and ignore it when he popped out naked in my presence? Why did I put up with any of it, even once?

What I wrote, and eventually published online in the *New York Review of Books*, opened with the following:

> Of all my assignments for Charlie Rose, the one that came with the oddest sense of happiness was when he asked that I unclog the toilet in the master bedroom of his Bellport home. It was brimming with feces and had left the upstairs smelling like a factory farm. My yellow dish gloves were flimsy and it was impossible to move the plunger without excrement slopping from the bowl. But I confidently reassured myself, *No man would ask this of a woman with whom he wanted to have sex.*

This happened in August 2007, a few months into my internship at his show. He had given me a paid side gig organizing the library of his Long Island estate's guesthouse, a job that required I stay multiple days isolated alone with him on his property. While plunging Charlie's bedroom toilet was unique among my experiences involving him, it was also symptomatic of most everything between us: I was obliging him in ways that I would never have expected of myself. I wasn't merely giving his behavior a pass; I was changing my own standards of appropriateness to accommodate for it—and as time went on, I would continue accommodating in ways far more detrimental to my well-being.

When people on social media responded to my story with outrage that a man would "force" a young female intern to perform such a demeaning task, I knew I had failed to accurately convey my message. Because for all of Charlie's ruthlessness, he would never "force" someone to unclog his toilet. Had I refused, sure, he'd have held a grudge. But he wouldn't have held a golf club to my head while suggesting I reconsider.

As I remember it, when he first broached the topic of the clogged toilet with me—how it couldn't be left to sit, but he needed to leave town—he appeared to have paused, as though briefly wondering, *Can I really ask this of her?* And I made absolutely sure that he could by giving the affirmative quickly, almost enthusiastically. Because however disgusting or degrading the task might sound to some, I welcomed it as an opportunity to prove categorically to his staff that I wasn't out to use my sex for professional gain. I was like so many other women I know who worked for misbehaving men: despite my boss's well-established reputation for impropriety, I wasn't nearly as scared of him as I was of people misinterpreting my own intentions. So before I put on my dish gloves, I texted the details of what I was undertaking to two employees with whom I'd become friends. I assumed the news would travel fast among the open-plan office, and I wanted it to. *What an insane story!* they would all laugh. *What an unflappable woman!* they would all think.

"Hi Charlie," I followed up in an email the next day. "After my best effort with the other plunger, it's still not working. I was wondering if you'd like me to call a plumber to come out?" His Bellport handyman had recommended one to me, I noted, but I was "happy to keep trying." How pitiful to be *forced* to unclog your lecherous boss's toilet, but how perverse to *want* to unclog it. I was far more comfortable in the latter camp. It was a version of the story in which I had control, and those are the kinds of stories we tell ourselves all the time, whether true or not.

The gap between rationally knowing something and truly understanding it is full of overly simplistic, reassuring stories, many of which overlook the chaos and cruelty of our world. Beyond making us feel safer, these stories serve our sense of self—our sense of free will and morality. When things get complicated or unfold antithetically to who we believe we are, they can envelop us like a dense fog, ensuring our heroism by clouding the most difficult of truths. But if we're willing to hold an unsettlingly bright light to ourselves, we can begin to illuminate the essence of these stories, and learn to see past them.

When I now hold that light to my experience with Charlie, I see some pretty fucked-up narratives about female acceptability and empowerment. I see the can-do independence of my 1980s American childhood, the sexualization of my 1990s adolescence, and a sinister mix of the two as a working woman of the aughts who was drowning in all the societal expectations and consumer culture that she thought she was above. I see the workplace abuse that I disregarded out of a misplaced pride in my own toughness, as well as my need for belonging. I see an almost blind deference to men whose narcissism I equated with aptitude, if not actual genius. My own fog had habituated me to norms and values that I had never truly questioned—not least of which was the personal status I had spent my life safeguarding as a white woman in a sexist and racist social hierarchy.

Put differently, I now see that I was *complicit*.

I do not use the word "complicit" lightly. I use it with all the heft it can carry—and with a brutal recognition that the soft power of the patriarchy had its way with me, inspiring me to undermine my own potential as well as that of other women. #MeToo changed many things, but it wasn't the paradigm shift we had hoped for. That's because what we're up against is more than powerful men and their powerful systems. We're up against our own psychological and cultural conditioning. We're up against all of Western history, society, literature, and mass media. We're up against habituation at its most pernicious—something so deep that it implicates us all, men and women, regardless of politics or good intentions. We haven't been *complacent* or *indifferent* or another tepid word that understates the nature and magnitude of the problem. We have been *complicit*.

"Ghostlike Forces"

To best understand our complicity, we need to begin by defining it. Or, rather, *re*defining it. We most often use the word "complicit" accusatorily while pointing a finger at someone for their *intentional* participation in harm. But the reality is that most people's conscious intentions are, from moment to moment, pretty benign. We're all just doing as best we can in imperfect circumstances, whatever our gender, social stature, or how others see us. The "bro" colleague who insists you're taking his sexist joke too seriously truly believes that your workweek would feel more humane if everyone could just let their guards down and assume the best of each other. The soulless HR rep who downplays a female colleague's report of harassment is someone struggling to serve multiple interests, including those of the executives upon whom her job rests. The CEO who cultivates an exclusive boys' club loves it when he sees himself in his company's young talent and only wishes he had more time to mentor in the same meaningful way that was done for him.

We are each the protagonist of our own story, in which none of us are the bad guy. Because unlike those whom we vilify, when it comes to our own lives, we have all the context necessary to justify our behavior. We shape our own narratives to overlook the less-than-heroic ways that we submit to those with power, condone abuse, or seek approval and personal gain. Or, for that matter, how we might not have been in the control we thought we were; how we ourselves may have been preyed upon.

Our complicity in any kind of injustice is at its most sinister when it's not intentional but unconscious. *This* is the complicity with which we're concerned. It happens in the narratives that shroud us, somewhere between our mindful intentions and our social conditioning; in the chasm between the freely choosing, empowered, self-aware, consistent, moral people we believe ourselves to be and the reality of our behavior—be it dumbfounded, daunted, uncertain, or oblivious. It's our fallback on assumptions and explanations that uphold our world as it too often is: misogynistic, racist, classist, homophobic, transphobic, xenophobic, ageist, exploitative, and otherwise fearful of the unknown. It's our internalized status quo—and all the cruelty that it leads us to tolerate.

In my exploration of our complicity, I've talked to more than one hundred people—women, men, nonbinary persons, victims, bystanders, and remorseful wrongdoers. The clearest thing to emerge from these conversations is how much we rely on overly simplistic stories to understand our complex lived experiences of sexual misconduct and workplace abuse more broadly. In fact, we rely on the same inadequate stories, all derived from the same patriarchal culture that has shaped our very consciousness. "Ghost-like forces that operate outside our awareness—with an initiation that bypasses conscious thought" is how the prominent developmental psychologist Carol Gilligan and the psychoanalyst Naomi Snider describe the enduring power of the patriarchy.[1] From a young age, we internalize patriarchal narratives that teach us appropriate male-versus-female behavior, the lines we must toe and the sacrifices we must make in order to belong. While this book focuses heavily on women's lived experiences, my hope is that male readers will understand their own relevance to the accounts of women in the following pages, whose struggles were formed, if not created, by the narratives men had of them—the constructs with which these women, in turn, had navigated their own lives.

When I use the term "patriarchal narrative," I'm referring broadly to any kind of story, explanation, assumption, or mode of thinking that works to justify the inequality inherent in our culture's gender binary—that leaves male entitlement and female subjugation the default social order. These narratives aren't good for anyone, and that very much includes men. They underlie an idealized version of masculinity that inspires emotional detachment and aggression, depriving men of meaningful relationships and love. They leave men isolated and alone, burdened by who they believe they must be in a reality that falls woefully short—financially, professionally, romantically—of what they have been shown to expect. In the United States, men are almost four times more likely to take their own lives than women, a disparity the American Psychological Association now decisively attributes to the toll that notions of traditional masculinity take on men.[2] The constraints and relentless pressures of our prescribed gender norms hurt *us all*.

The collective nature of our suffering was evidenced by news stories about sexual harassment giving way to stories about abusive bosses, giving way to stories about toxic work cultures that crushed the well-being of both women and men. Along the way, we did more than broaden our understanding of professional misconduct: we saw the consequences of gender socialization in our hyperindividualistic, ultracompetitive patriarchy. We saw that our professional hierarchies mirror our social ones, with the same *ghostlike forces* bringing the unthinkable to pass in our workplaces.

Of course, for many people who endure workplace abuse, there is nothing seemingly supernatural about it; they suffer with a keen awareness of the power dynamics and cruelty at play, and because they simply have no other option. A service worker and single mother who endures her boss's wandering hands may do so because reporting him would jeopardize the ability to feed her children. There is little appeal to seeking recourse when the risks are so enormous. But what about the ambitious new paralegal with Ivy League credentials and a trust fund who downplays her superior's pervy misbehavior because she says she can "handle it"? She would arguably have an easier time doing differently, and yet she doesn't. It's for good reason that the personal accounts in this book focus on women who are like me: educated, white, straight, and cisgender. With relatively more resources and protections at our disposal than on average, our experiences can inform us about how subtle, unconscious misogyny sustains the existing power structure. It's a simple truism that a society's most advantaged individuals are also its least inclined to question the norm.

What the Black feminist scholar bell hooks called an "imperialist white supremacist capitalist patriarchy" may sound abstract to some, but the benefits it bestows on women like me could not be more concrete.[3] Sure, the system subjugates us. But it also rewards our obedience in ways denied to people of color, and in ways to which we can remain comfortably blind. We use our patriarchal narratives to effortlessly craft a sense of self in which our rank is God-given. We don't question it when we're told during a job interview that we'd be a "good fit." We don't question it when our rental application gets accepted amid a housing crisis, or years later when we access a mortgage. We don't question the vision we have of our future, because we've never *not* seen celebrated representations of women who look like us. And we certainly don't question the romantic ideals around which we've structured and too often compromised our lives, because courtship and marriage are our guaranteed proximity to true power. Not every white woman is a so-called Karen, but that doesn't spare her from being a cog in a racist system that works to her benefit.

Still, it demands emphasis that no matter a victim's race or social stature, they are not to be blamed for their abuse. To recognize how women are conditioned to enable their own mistreatment and to blame them for said mistreatment are two entirely different things. This distinction—and the understanding that this book in no way seeks to victim blame—is the most critical request that I make of the reader. It's an ask that will understandably make some uncomfortable. They might wonder: Why do *anything* that risks calling women's behavior into question when such questioning is the very MO that has kept them down for millennia? Their concern is well-taken.

#MeToo did not change the reality that we live in a rape culture that puts the onus on women to know how to avoid becoming a statistic. Self-proclaimed misogynistic influencers like Andrew Tate, who has millions of devoted young male followers, broadcast that women bear responsibility for their own assaults. High-profile women who accuse high-profile domestic partners of abuse, regardless of the credibility or absolute horror of what they claim, receive a level of online hate so staggering that it negatively impacts advocacy on behalf of *all* domestic violence victims. When it comes to our justice system's handling of rape, women are doubted or blamed from the moment they report the crime. Alleged assailants go free in forty-nine out of every fifty such cases, which makes rape easier to get away with than robbery.[4] And when it comes to convicting someone of sexual harassment, our courts require that the conduct in question be shown to have been "unwelcome"—inevitably putting the legal focus on the behavior and dress of female plaintiffs in an effort to determine if they had actually "wanted it."[5]

Yet while victim blaming is a culturally and institutionally entrenched part of our lives, at its most insidious it happens in the fog of our self-serving narratives. It's an ever-so-subtle presumption that we make about other people's weaknesses relative to our own protagonism. *I would have shut him up*, we think. Or *I would have walked out*. Or *I would never have gone along in the first place*. We do this because if it can be their fault, we won't have to contemplate our own vulnerability in a misogynistic and arbitrarily cruel world. We can instead maintain a fundamental sense of assurance that we're in control of our own lives. The service that victim blaming provides our emotional and mental well-being is so vital that we'll even blame those with whom we empathize dearly.

Everyone has a faith in their own hypothetical ability to handle creeps and sticky situations. But if you're like me, you've had the opportunity to learn that what happens in real time, under pressure and disparate power dynamics, doesn't always play out how you would have imagined. Perhaps, also like me, you moved on in whatever way helped your immediate well-being, sometimes suppressing an honest recognition of what exactly transpired. None of us are as self-aware or reliable as we think we are. This is a difficult truth to recognize in normal circumstances—and far more difficult when confronting indignity and injustice. But to embrace it is to create an opportunity for true empowerment. It's to see our own internalized patriarchy with the nuance necessary to begin dismantling it.

Women, of course, have agency and power, and untold numbers of them have immediately identified and called out their own sexist mistreatment, despite the repercussions that awaited them. Legions more have handled unwanted advances successfully, indeed brilliantly. I, however, did not. Not with Charlie, nor with far too many other men I've had the displeasure of meeting. Time and again, I was hamstrung by my own most trusted attributes: friendliness, amenability, deference, and self-deprecation—the traits I had leaned hard on throughout my personal and professional life. But the more I've talked about my blind spots and the confusing, ensnaring aspects of these encounters, the more I've tapped into something vital. Women have related most earnestly to what I originally assumed would only discredit me, and often to what brought me the most shame. They, too, had sent sycophantic emails to creepy, egomaniacal bosses. They, too, had continued smiling and bantering with their perpetrators. They, too, interpreted their own silence as encouragement. They, too, continued going to work, too stunned and exhausted to fully acknowledge, even to themselves, what was happening.

For each of the thirty-five women to date who went on the record against Charlie, I believe there are myriad more who kept quiet. Like me, they struggled to understand what had happened. Maybe, in the beginning, they had enjoyed the company of a highly regarded cultural icon and responded politely to his flirtations. Maybe it felt like the appropriate, courteous response to a man of his age and stature. They tolerated it because their tolerance made him happy, because they understood from others that this was his nature, but most of all because it was easy—far, far easier than asking perhaps the most influential man they had ever met to respect boundaries. They acquiesced so that they could go on working. Sometimes it was lousy, but other times it was fine, occasionally quite professional. Until one day, without warning, he became aggressively physical and the line these women already felt uncomfortable for having blurred got completely erased. *Did I cause this?* they wondered. *How do I stop it without upsetting him?* As they struggled for answers, and as their so-called consent escaped them, the only thing that came into clarity was their own disposability.

Within our quest to not blame victims—and to ensure that we women are finally believed instead of mocked, vilified, or shunned—we've avoided scrutinizing our encounters in a way that can shed greater light on the sources of our vulnerability. In the early years of the #MeToo movement, and as powerful men fell from the greatest of heights, events seemed so earth-shattering that any such exploration felt unnecessary, if not insulting to the victims who had been brave enough to speak out. But if the years since have proved anything, it's that our supposed reckoning was not seismic. At the time of this writing, the same pussy-grabber who inspired the 2017 Women's March is the clear front-runner for the 2024 GOP presidential nomination. Only this time he has been found liable for sexual abuse, and faces a slew of other damning charges in four separate criminal cases.[6] Nothing captures our fidelity to male entitlement quite like U.S. presidential politics.

Polling now indicates that levels of sexism in our society have remained stable, if not worsened, in a counterreaction to #MeToo.[7] During the pandemic, workplace harassment surged with the increase of remote work as barriers were blurred between our private and professional lives.[8] Most concerning is that data indicate an insidious backlash, showing that while the most egregious kinds of sexual harassment that tend to garner our attention—like threatening forms of sexual coercion—may have gone down, more subtle forms of gender harassment—like inappropriate remarks about women and the undermining of their work—have actually increased. This latter kind of harassment not only feeds the former, but its frequent ability to evade the categorical definitions of illegal behavior also makes it more difficult to combat. It accounts for the lion's share of all sexual harassment. It's pervasive, ostracizing to women, and can be equally if not more damaging to their well-being than unwanted sexual advances or sexual coercion.[9] "Death by a thousand cuts," I heard time and again from women about their hostile environments. "If it had only been his hands, I'd have managed," said one.

Nor does it help that most of the approaches used by our workplaces to combat sexual harassment and discrimination don't actually deliver. When sociologists examined the impact of sexual harassment training policies at more than eight hundred U.S. companies with more than eight million employees over a span of thirty-two years, they found that mandatory training tended to only make male employees more likely to blame female victims—to accuse them of either overreacting or concocting a false story. According to researchers, identifying male colleagues as potential perpetrators rarely strikes a productive tone—certainly not in a world where none of us believes that we're the bad guy. "Start *any* training by telling a group of people that they're the problem, and they'll get defensive," researchers write. "Once that happens, they're much less likely to want to be a part of the solution; instead they'll resist."[10]

Many point to bystander intervention training—equipping employees with methods to intervene when they see harassment happening—as the more promising option. But this approach is far from a silver bullet. It reduces the problem down to a few bad apples whom we can supposedly learn how to stop while overlooking the kind of situational complexity that most often gives rise to bad behavior.[11] As this book will examine, our actions—as well as our inaction—are powerfully driven by social context. Workplace policies and the intentions behind them are critical. But our offices are microcosms of the larger world in which we all live, and as the pioneering social ecologist Peter Drucker warned: "Culture eats strategy for breakfast."[12]

Meaningful change demands exorcising the ghostlike forces of the patriarchy. This can only begin by more fully examining the complexity of our lived experiences relative to the overly simplistic narratives that we use to explain them—even, and especially, when the reality we confront is unsettling.

When Sean Penn came to the defense of his good pal Charlie Rose in May 2018, he criticized the #MeToo movement for being "not intellectually honest," saying, "I know of some serious omissions. I'm talking about women towards men."[13] I agree that details were omitted—and continue being omitted with every story that has broken since about powerful people sexually harassing, abusing, or exploiting others. Overlooked details can be added not in defense of the perpetrators or to delegitimize the victims but to expand our awareness of how implicated we all are in the sexism and injustice we believe we stand against. What follows is an attempt to do just that.

CHAPTER ONE

The High Price of Our Free Will

"It is your decisions, and not your conditions, that determine your destiny."

So says America's most famous life coach, Tony Robbins. The six-foot-seven California native teaches his followers to unleash their inner power and take control of their lives—often at coaching sessions they've paid thousands of dollars to attend. Audio and video recordings are forbidden at these events, but a video leaked in April 2018 in which Robbins broadly dismissed women's #MeToo allegations as misguided attempts to find significance by attacking other people. When a female attendee stood up to challenge this description, he pushed back. "I'm not knocking the #MeToo movement," he insisted. "I'm knocking victimhood." He asked his audience to raise a hand if they understood. Cheers erupted in the auditorium, signaling a deep appreciation for what is perhaps Robbins's most compelling message: victimhood is a choice.[1]

Outside the auditorium, the public was less receptive. Robbins eventually apologized for suggesting anything other than "profound admiration" for the #MeToo movement, adding that he was committed to being part of the solution.[2] But the skills of a self-help guru don't easily parlay into success at ending systemic injustice. Eight months later, Robbins was again secretly recorded during a six-day Date with Destiny seminar in Palm Beach, Florida. In the recording, a female attendee speaks softly about her husband emotionally abusing her. "She *likes* to call it emotional abuse," Robbins tells his audience. "What the fuck is emotional abuse? Are we that fucking weak that someone can't tell you with passion what they fucking feel without them abusing you?"[3]

The woman goes on to clarify that she's also been physically abused by her husband. Robbins asks her what role she played in that abuse, changing the paradigm, presumably to help her take responsibility for the situation. "I'm not suggesting there's *any* excuse for hitting a woman, so hear me, but I also want you to know that people don't just act a certain fucking way," he says, explaining that sometimes, when people don't like a given behavior, they decide to relabel it as abuse. "She's lying to herself," he tells the audience. "She's done it so often, she doesn't even know the difference between a truth and a lie anymore."[4]

This no-nonsense message of self-empowerment hinges upon a deep faith in personal agency—a belief that most of our suffering is entirely in our power to fix—if, of course, we have the determination to do so; if we have the willpower to overcome the internal obstacles and bad mental habits that keep us down. Robbins continues to reframe the story by asking the woman about her husband: "Has he looked out for you? Does he put up with you when you've been a crazy bitch? Have you ever been a crazy bitch? Ever?"

"Probably, yes," she says, her voice trembling. The audience laughs.[5] Some might see this as tough love. Others might call it victim blaming.

The leaked recording was published by *BuzzFeed News* in 2019 as part of an investigation into a number of allegations against Robbins, including berating female victims of domestic violence and rape; targeting, hitting on, and inappropriately touching female attendees at his events; and subjecting female staff to nudity and unwanted sexual advances.[6] Robbins has strenuously denied all the allegations. (He's also filed defamation suits in the Irish high court against *Buzz-Feed News* for its reporting and Twitter—now X—for distributing said reporting, in a brazen move that some call "libel tourism.")[7] But even then, not all the women who spoke on the record minded his behavior. One former employee explained that, although he could make her feel demeaned by, say, staring at her breasts, his teachings had helped her not to see herself as a victim: "While I may not agree with everything Tony does as a person, I am forever grateful for the gift Tony's been in my life."[8] And as for the "crazy bitch" in the recording, she said that he empowered her to find her own agency, with which she finally left her husband. In a video she posted on YouTube, she described the encounter she had with Robbins as a "sacred moment"—right before plugging the self-help book she had since written on finding real love and fulfillment.[9]

Tony Robbins wouldn't have a net worth of $600 million were he not tapping into our most fundamental need: the need to feel that we're entirely in control of our own lives and our own outcomes. But if, as he says, it's our decisions and not our conditions that determine our destiny, we should at least acknowledge how much our conditions determine our decisions. More specifically, the cultural conditions of a Western society that has a foundational belief in free will and in the power and potential of every individual.

We enter the world being told that within each of us resides the boundless capacity to *do* and *be* whatever we want. It's an essential, powerful, positively affecting message that helps us to get out of bed day in and day out. But when taken to an extreme, it entices us to perceive systemic social problems as a question of individual aptitude—of one's strength, savvy, or goodness. Injustice becomes about personal failure in a world where we all get what we deserve.

What makes our culture so potently hostile to women is that it's more than sexist; it's extremely individualistic. Despite gender inequality—as well as racial and economic inequality—people are assumed to be where they are based on the fortitude of their individual character far more than the reality of their circumstances. In recent years the #MeToo movement, Black Lives Matter, and the Covid pandemic left many questioning our long-held narratives of what exactly one can *will* to happen. All our decisions, determination, and hard work can get us only so far when inequity is baked into the system. But more relevant to our own enabling of cruelty and abuse is that our free will is also undercut powerfully by our cultural and social contexts. In fact, our behavior is influenced in every circumstance of every day by external factors beyond our immediate awareness.

What I heard most in reporting for this book was some variation of the phrase "I always thought of myself as . . ." Indeed, we had all generally thought of ourselves as moral, capable, objective, discerning, responsible people with firm boundaries. But then we got the opportunity to either experience or be a bystander to workplace abuse, and it turned out that we didn't behave as we would have expected. Recall that the kind of complicity we're concerned with is unintentional: it's about what we've been conditioned to do or overlook. To understand it demands deconstructing our thinking and parsing out all the harmful falsehoods and illusions that have seeped into it. At a very deep level, we create and cling to overly simplistic explanations—indeed reassurances—for our behavior. That's why far more important than "he said, she said" is what we said to ourselves, and all the reasons we said it.

Every chapter of this book is devoted to an inconvenient truth that's necessary to confront before we can meaningfully address not just our enablement of misbehaving men but our complicity in sexual misconduct and workplace abuse more broadly. These are deeply rooted cultural and psychological tendencies that are resistant to change, regardless of generation, professional industry, or newly implemented HR practices. They're the patriarchal narratives and defense mechanisms that we fall back on when our sense of self or well-being is threatened. They're the stories that keep us confined to a status quo of inequality.

In what follows, some of the names and identifying details have been changed. We begin with the myth of our categorical, unflinching free will.

Ugh. Why Did You Do That?

The kind of victim blaming we're most familiar with is the textbook, villainous kind—what Harvey Weinstein's defense lawyer Donna Rotunno demonstrated in an interview with the *New York Times* podcast *The Daily*. Megan Twohey, one of the newspaper's reporters who broke the initial story on Weinstein's abuses, asked Rotunno if she had ever been sexually assaulted. "I have not, because I would never put myself in that position," she said. "I've always made choices, from college age on, where I never drank too much, I never went home with someone that I didn't know. I just never put myself in any vulnerable circumstance ever."[10]

One might think that Rotunno was *trying* to stoke outrage—which she did. "There's a Special Place in Hell for Harvey Weinstein's Lawyer," read a *New York* magazine headline. "Do NOT listen to the @nytimes The Daily podcast interview with Weinstein's defense lawyer Donna Rotunno unless you want to levitate with rage," tweeted mom blogger Whitney Cicero.[*] Former CBS reporter Kate Smith asked, "How is this 2020?"[†] (Sadly, misogynistic tropes would hardly be the most difficult thing to believe about 2020.)

Yet, for all the indignation and disgust, Rotunno's remark—and her belief that she herself had the savvy and wherewithal to avoid harm—is merely a more candid demonstration of a kind of self-confidence upon which we all rely. While I may have gasped in horror when I first heard Rotunno's comment, I've since become less offended. Not because I've developed a tolerance for flagrant victim blaming, but because I've been forced to develop a humility about my own such tendencies. In fact, over the course of reporting for this book, I repeatedly found myself doing my own victim blaming, often uncontrollably, and in a way that's actually far more insidious than Rotunno's standard fare.

By now you know that when confronted with Charlie's advances, I failed spectacularly at being the woman I thought I was. Pretty much nothing played out as I would have expected of myself. Yet over the past few years, when listening to women tell me about their own similar experiences—women for whom I have deep empathy and respect—something sometimes uncontrollably clicked on in the back of my mind. It was a sort of mental simulation, like a *Choose Your Own Adventure: Sexual Misconduct*, which I could have only

---

[*] Cicero's tweet has since been deleted. I last read it on X in February 2023.

[†] Kate Smith's account has since been made private.

been playing out of a belief that I would choose to do differently than these women. And thus I would have avoided the same fate. I'm confident that Rotunno and I have very different views on the causes and significance of sexual abuse, but we use the same mental pattern for processing the topic as it relates to us personally.

The first woman I caught myself blaming for her own abuse was a theater director named Kim Rubinstein, who told me all about her experience working for a sexually predatory boss at the Long Wharf Theatre in New Haven, Connecticut. As I always did at the beginning of an interview, I assured her that nothing would be used without her permission. But Rubinstein was a fearlessly open book and quick to set the terms: "You can ask me anything," she said. "Nothing is off-limits. We can go *anywhere*."[11] She had found everything about her experience confounding, and in ways that she felt needed to be acknowledged in order to bring about greater awareness. "For people on the outside, it's so cut-and-dry," she told me. "But in the moment, it can be so destabilizing and confusing."

Rubinstein described her boss as both manipulative and persistent: He would forcibly kiss and grope her and press himself against her whenever closed doors allowed. She would push him off her or ignore him, but that didn't stop him from coming into her office and masturbating while she worked at her computer, after which he'd sit grinning at her with semen on his shirttails. I nodded along as she told me about the people she had turned to for help, and how they were either reluctant or unable to do anything. I even teared up a bit when she spoke devastatingly of the professional opportunities she lost by leaving her job at the Long Wharf. But then she mentioned the times when she gave in to his demands for sex, hoping it could give her a reprieve. And that's when I felt it and first identified it: the sensation of empathy morphing into pity, into judgment. Were I to give the feeling syntax, it might be: *Ugh. Why did you do that?*

In that moment, possibly the darkest, most upsetting part of Rubinstein's story, I needed to feel removed from the kind of threat and circumstances she was describing—I needed her misfortune to remain inapplicable to my own life. And fixating on her behavior allowed me to do exactly that. By locating and containing the problem in her, I didn't have to feel it touching me. That's how I took an instance of sexual abuse in a misogynistic world and transformed it into a story about free will and bad choices.

Not long after my conversation with Rubinstein, my family's dearly loved babysitter told me that a man had torn a purse with two weeks' pay from her hands while she was walking home the night before. My very first thought was about how late she had been out—during a pandemic, no less—and my second was about her tendency to meander lost in her thoughts. My mind did not immediately go to either of the two times that I've been mugged—moments that rank among the most helpless I've ever felt in my life, after which I was afraid for months to walk alone on the street after dark. As with Rubinstein, I knew all too well what my babysitter had gone through. Even worse, it may have been precisely *because* I knew that my immediate reaction was to identify behavior worthy of blame.

In 1965, the social psychologist Melvin J. Lerner wanted to study how people come to accept government regimes and social norms that result in horrible suffering. He devised an experiment in which seventy-two female volunteer student participants were broken into smaller groups and shown a closed-circuit video of a woman enduring physical pain. The woman was presented as another volunteer, though in reality she was a graduate student collaborating in the study. She had electrodes attached to her head, and participants were told that she would be asked questions and given electric shocks for each incorrect answer provided. As with Stanley Milgram's famous shock experiment earlier that decade, the study's participants watched as she gave wrong answers, screamed, and writhed in (pretend) pain.[12]

Lerner provided one group of participants the option to stop the torture and continue instead using positive reinforcements—which most of them opted to do. When asked about the female volunteer who took the test, these participants generally described her as an innocent victim. Another group of volunteers, however, was given no such option to change the woman's circumstances. And as her torture proceeded, he told them various stories: that she was being paid for her participation, that she was doing it for free, or that she had voluntarily opted to continue being tortured after being told that the study's other participants (i.e., those watching) would be denied necessary lab credits should she stop. In the end, the less they thought she was being compensated for the suffering, the *more* the participants disliked her, and the more they faulted her for not giving the correct answers. She was blamed the most by her female peers in the scenario where they believed she was voluntarily being tortured for the benefit of the group.[13]

The more we define ourselves as freely choosing individuals, capable of determining our own fates, the easier it becomes to explain cruelty as somehow caused by the victim. By extension, the more we put the responsibility on women to protect their own well-being in a patriarchal world, the more culpable they will be judged in their own abuse. Such judgment, we know, often manifests as the casual perception of female wantonness. When young female interns at *Charlie Rose* agreed to work with him from his Bellport estate or fly with him on a private plane to help him interview someone illustrious, those of us on staff seemed to assume one of two things about these women: they either had control of the situation or they were game for whatever he might try. In this way, we didn't have to concern ourselves with their fate. But worse than that, I look back now and see how quick I was to write a couple of these young women off as "wanting it," merely because they seemed too bubbly around Charlie. I have no idea what their experiences were, only that my judgment of them was deeply hypocritical. I made such an assumption despite knowing that I myself had never once "wanted it." But I wasn't ready to comprehend the injustice of it all, nor stomach how I had been affected personally.

After his research, Lerner concluded that "the sight of an inno-cent person suffering without possibility of reward or compensation motivated people to devalue the attractiveness of the victim in order to bring about a more appropriate fit between her fate and her character."[14] From this insight, he developed what's called the "just-world hypothesis," a tendency to believe that people get more or less what they deserve in a world that's essentially orderly and fair. To be truly heedful of the opposite—to spend our daily lives mindful of how easily terrible things can befall absolutely anyone for no other reason than shit happens—is a painfully distressing way to live. So distressing, in fact, that we'll even opt to blame ourselves unfairly before embracing the unpredictable cruelty of our world.

Consider the experience of an attorney in Oregon named Mer-edith Holley. In 2014, Holley was thirty-two years old and starting a new job with a law firm known for civil rights litigation. As an associate attorney, she would be representing plaintiffs in discrim-ination cases, many of which involved sexual harassment. Holley was thrilled for this professional opportunity and eager to prove herself. But among the colleagues she had intended to impress was a partner who touched her unnecessarily on a daily basis and made comments that ranged from flirtatious to demeaning. Once, while stopping by her office, he took a piece of chocolate from a jar of candy atop her desk for visitors. He unwrapped it, took a bite, and told her: "You're sweet like the chocolate. But I know how the chocolate tastes, while I don't know . . ." His words trailed into excruciating silence.

How did Holley, a self-described feminist trained to address illegal discrimination, respond to such obvious sexual harassment? By blaming herself. "I would never have said it at the time, but I had an underlying assumption that there's something wrong with me—that I was creating his behavior," she said. "I'm wearing the wrong dress. I talk too loud. I talk too soft. I giggle too much. I didn't tell him no—all of these things that I would never think about anyone else."[15]

A chance to change her thinking came when Holley began a concerted effort to walk more. She started listening to audio books on her walk to work, including those of the Tibetan Buddhist teacher Pema Chödrön, whose counsel on matters of discomfort and uncertainty often emphasizes compassion. With an interest already sparked in nonorthodox frames of mind, Holley added podcasts to her walks that were about the power of understanding our thoughts—their origins, and their impacts on our feelings and self-regard. It wasn't long until she enrolled in a course on the topic and, by learning to better identify and understand her own thoughts, began to address what she called her own "internalized misogyny."

"We get programmed with these oppressive thought patterns that to most of us just look normal. And it creates a system where the people who are advantaged by oppression don't even have to work at it, because we'll do it for them—we'll self-oppress," she explained. This can be the job we're quick to assume we're not qualified for, the raise we're unsure we merit, the statement we're afraid won't add value, or the workplace respect and dignity we figure we don't deserve. Holley believes that her harasser's actual intentions were nothing in comparison to the self-loathing with which she responded to his behavior. "He was abusing me, but then I was like, *Hold my beer! I'll do it better than you!*"

Only after Holley was able to truly believe that she wasn't at fault for her harassment did things improve. She described becoming more confident and more effective at communicating, which she says did more to stop the harassment than reporting him to her superiors had done. She made it clear to her perpetrator and other colleagues capable of intervening that certain behavior was unacceptable and needed to change. When she pushed back against her own ghostlike forces of the patriarchy, the entire script was disrupted—not just hers. Her experience in overcoming self-blame was powerful enough to inspire her to start her own conflict-resolution practice focused on toxic workplaces. Today she helps train other women, men, and nonbinary people to address their own harassment, along with their own internalized misogyny.

I asked her about her work with these women, and if she thought victimhood was in any way a choice. She smiled. "We're taught to think about victimhood in a binary way: either it's all our fault or our world is hopelessly beyond our control," she told me. "But there's a range in that binary space where we can say, *There are things in my control and things not in my control. His actions are not my fault and there are still things that I can do differently to make this environment safer.* But it's weirdly challenging mentally, and it takes courage because you have to imagine doing things that are not normal for a woman in our culture."

It's easier to assume that we simply failed and that things can be managed correctly the next time than to recognize how conditioned we've been to acquiesce to men. As #MeToo unfolded, women were quoted in the news referring to their "*Matrix* moment," a reference to the scene in the movie when Neo accepts Morpheus's red pill. He wakes up to discover that he's lived his entire life in a simulated reality built by machine overlords that have been harvesting his body in the service of their own domination. It was an apt metaphor for a patriarchal world in which our submission is by design.* But as any fan of the franchise knows, cautiously surviving in grottos under the surface of an incinerated planet is sometimes a hard sell. The Matrix beckons its beleaguered defectors to plug back in, where they can again live relatively stress-free, enjoying creature comforts like a nice glass of wine. It's a similarly agonizing slog to live with a constant awareness of our patriarchal society's cruelty and what it takes from each of us. So we opt out. And when things go wrong, we do what the system has programmed us to do: look inward for answers.

"Bitch, You Don't Know How to Hang Up a Phone?"

In 2003, Abby Schachner phoned fellow comedian Louis C.K. to invite him to her upcoming comedy show. He began making lewd

---

* The metaphor is especially apt for transgender people as well, who question their own reality before choosing the difficult and dangerous act of living according to their authentic selves. In fact, at the time the movie was made in 1999, the red pill that Morpheus offers Neo resembled the estrogen pills used in hormone replacement therapy. Two decades later, Lilly Wachowski, who wrote and directed the franchise with her sister Lana Wachowski, acknowledged that the Matrix was indeed a trans allegory—as some had long speculated. Lana and Lilly themselves came out as trans in 2010 and 2016, respectively.

conversation and was soon, unmistakably, masturbating over the phone. When Schachner became one of five women in 2017 to accuse C.K. of inappropriate conduct that he would later acknowledge took place, she had explained to the *New York Times* that she found the phone call professionally discouraging.[16]

A month after that, on his new Netflix special, another comedian, Dave Chappelle, posed a question for Schachner: "Bitch, you don't know how to hang up a phone? How the fuck are you going to survive in show business if this is an actual obstacle to your dreams?" Profanity and misogyny aside, Chapelle was expressing a problem that many people had with the #MeToo movement: Couldn't so many of the women who had spoken out done differently? Why didn't they say no, get up and leave, or file an HR report? What about personal responsibility? Personal agency? Free will? Some of this stuff just didn't make sense. And the easiest way to *make* it make sense was by drawing conclusions about the character of the women involved.

Regardless of what we might think of Chappelle's rant or his views on sexual misconduct, we all tend to interpret people's behavior as something done with mindful intention and not out of situational necessity—as a reflection of a person's character and not their circumstances. It's a cognitive bias that permeates our understanding of others as we constantly make what psychologists call "dispositional inferences" about why people do what they do. We see the colleague who misses a deadline as unreliable when maybe he's been overtasked. The guy who just cut in front of us at the café counter is a jerk, not possibly confused by the line's haphazard shape. The mom who hands the iPhone to her toddler is willfully negligent, not in dire need of a break, however she can snag it.

These kinds of judgments about people's personalities, motives, beliefs, etc., *could* have veracity to them. More often than not, we can't confirm precisely why others do the things they do. And yet, when it comes to our own actions, we know with certainty that we're just doing as best we can, and *we* get a pass. Nobody understands the challenges or constraints of our own lives better than we ourselves do. "People generally think that their own behavior is largely a matter of responding sensibly to the situation they happen to be in—whether that behavior is admirable or abominable," writes Richard Nisbett, one of America's most influential academic psychologists.[17] Nisbett has extensively studied the dispositional inferences we make, with his research showing that the inclination to judge based on character and not context is far more common in individualistic Western societies like our own. Our counterparts in Asian societies, for example, who tend to see things more in terms of interdependence and social harmony, have a greater sensitivity to situational pressures and make fewer judgments about the character of their peers.

In one study, Korean and American students were given a politically opinionated essay to read and told that the author had "no choice" about what to write. Students from both cultures erred in the assumption that the writer believed the essay's argument. But after both groups then had to write their own essays arguing an opinion assigned to them by the study's administrators, the Korean students were quick to revise their original perception of the author and their motivation for writing what they had written. Meanwhile, the American students stuck to their initial presumption that the writer was advocating their true feelings. The link between personal beliefs and personal behavior remained unchanged for the Americans, despite having just experienced for themselves how easily the two could be detached.[18]

Another of Nisbett's studies showed an identical underwater animation to students at both the University of Michigan and Kyoto University in Japan, who were then asked to describe what they saw. The Japanese students began with the setting—the rocks at the bottom of the pond, the color of the water—and were attentive to interactions among the wildlife. They gave 70 percent more responses about the environmental context than their U.S. counterparts, who quickly focused on the biggest fish, the fastest fish, or the brightest object.[19]

Some cultural anthropologists have expressed discomfort with Nisbett's broad conclusions about billions of people he lumps together as "East Asian." For our purposes, however, his work illuminates something critical about the stories we use to understand professional misconduct here in the West, which is that we have a hard time pulling back to see the whole of the ecosystem. By 2019, polling indicated that perspectives on gender, power, and sexual misconduct had shifted and that more people were seeing what they thought was part of a larger, serious problem.[20] But even as we expanded our awareness of the circumstances at play—even as we learned about the institutional power differentials, the nondisclosure agreements, the ruthlessness of our workplace cultures, the career-crushing price of seeking recourse, etc.—what changed most was *whose* character we focused on. Because the simple truth is that people are always better than situational factors at commanding our attention.[21]

When #MeToo happened, fixating on the character of famous male wrongdoers actually seemed like a noble thing to do, a necessary foray behind the smoke screen. When for so long the character of women who accused high-profile men of sexual abuse had been maligned, be they "conniving whores" or "wanton bimbos," it was now our responsibility to see the ghastly images of these perpetrators from atop their perches. They preferred their pedicures sans underwear and in short shorts, airing their genitals in the faces of salon staff, as casino magnate Steve Wynn is said to have done regularly. They lived lives of bone-chilling hypocrisy, like New York attorney general Eric Schneiderman, who while leading the charge against powerful men who committed sexual assault was himself slapping and choking the women he dated to the point that they reported needing medical attention. NBC's Matt Lauer was like a sadistic Mr. Burns, allegedly trapping women in his office with the simple press of a secret desk button. Chef Mario Batali's safe space for assaulting women was said to be on the third floor of the Spotted Pig gastropub in the West Village, in what had been dubbed by its staff as the "rape room." And by the time we found out in 2021 that a prominent Middle-earth monster's face in the *Lord of the Rings* movie trilogy had, decades prior, been modeled after Harvey Weinstein's own contorted blob of a mug, we weren't surprised.[22] These were exceptionally vivid villains.

But did the vilification of any of the perpetrators empower their victims? And as we took care to listen to women, did believing them credible equate to true change? The personal experience of Abby Schachner, who continued talking to C.K. as he masturbated over the phone, is an example of how our character-driven explanations can fail women regardless of who gets vilified. When I spoke with her, Schachner explained that she was never eager to tell her story. She did so only to lend credibility to her friends and fellow comedians Dana Min Goodman and Julia Wolov, who had committed to going on the record in the *New York Times* with the accusation that C.K. had masturbated nude in front of them at a comedy festival in Colorado. Schachner had never once considered

herself a victim, preferring instead the term "unfortunate recipient."
In fact, she felt a certain level of complicity in the now-infamous
2003 phone call. "I felt like I was part of it. I *did* stay on the phone.
I *did* indulge it—just not in a sexual way," she told me.

Her story contained an important recurring theme in my conversations with women, which was that their perpetrator's behavior
was said and done before they could adequately process it or craft
an intentioned response. Schachner never had the opportunity to
act with actual willfulness because she was sideswiped and then
two steps behind the entire time, with the thought of hanging up
or telling him to stop not even entering her mind until the conversation was over.

For context, prior to the call, Schachner had considered C.K. a
friend and mentor. He'd been among the first people in the industry
to express an interest in her writing, and when she bumped into
him years after their first contact, at a comedy club in Los Angeles,
they were happy to see each other. They exchanged numbers and
she called him a few days later. In the moments that she could hear
C.K. drawing the blinds, and as he began sharing a sexual fantasy,
Schachner didn't feel a sense of offense or disgust. Instead, she
described having a sense that *she could handle it*—that she could
manage C.K. while still maintaining cordiality and not losing her cool.

It's often the case that when a woman is made to feel uncomfortable by a male acquaintance, she will respond by doubling down
on protecting his ego and preserving the relationship's normal tenor,
even at her own expense.[23] So Schachner did what one does in
comedy: she rolled with it. "I was trying to be entertaining. Not
to be sexual or to encourage it but just to kind of try to keep up
with it. It was like, *I'm a comedian! I can do this!*" She proceeded
to talk—a lot—and to share awkward, embarrassing stories that

she had never shared with anyone. It was one big, surreal improv, and once it had started, Schachner wasn't sure how to stop. Only after C.K. had finished and began to shoo her off the phone did the reality of exactly what had just transpired hit her.

When she went on the record, Schachner sought to give the story of her encounter with C.K. nuance and ample context—although she would soon realize how little control she had over the narrative after it went public. "I told the *New York Times* that Louis was one of the *many* reasons I'm not in the business anymore," she pointed out, explaining that the story as it initially ran used a more categorical description of him having discouraged her from pursuing comedy. The paragraph in question was then screenshotted and tweeted by a presumably well-intentioned Judd Apatow, who wrote: "This to me was one of the saddest parts of the Louis CK story . . . When you disrespect and sexually harass young, vulnerable people you become a dream killer."[24]

Schachner was confused and upset by this and so many of the reactions that followed. There are women whose career aspirations could be derailed by one bad encounter, but that wasn't what happened. She said the experience with C.K. never extinguished her creativity and that there was no single explanation for her career trajectory. "I'm not going to blame *one* person for why I'm not doing something. It's a series of things, you know?" Other women I interviewed echoed Schachner's frustration that the reporting of their mistreatment had been reductive, while some declined to speak with me for fear that I'd similarly whittle their experience down to hapless victimhood. "I can't even read the story," one said about the initial exposé on her boss's sexual harassment. "I sound so pathetic and naive in it."

I know well that it's not fun having an intensely personal, fraught experience told by others. I also know that reporting stories comes with editorial constraints and that it's not a journalist's job to detail the entirety of what a source would like people to read. But beyond all of this is that "just the facts," however validating they are to a woman's story, can still feel to her like a disservice. And it turns out there's something to that feeling.

In 2019, a team at the Carnegie Mellon University School of Computer Science's Language Technologies Institute analyzed 27,602 English-language news stories related to #MeToo drawn from 1,576 media outlets. The articles, published between November 2017 and May 2018, were examined for hidden or veiled biases—the subtle, more difficult to detect ways that articles had portrayed women and their accused harassers. More specifically, researchers wanted to understand how individuals were depicted in terms of their inherent power, agency, and relatability.[25] They did this by mapping the verbs used, accounting for both the literal meaning and the context. (The verb "deserve," for example, has a different connotation in "He deserves the benefit of the doubt" versus "He deserves consequences.") Data showed that although stories were generally sympathetic to women who had experienced sexual harassment, the women were overwhelmingly portrayed as having less agency than men and significantly less power. The men were consistently presented as powerful, even after accusations had been leveraged; they remained strong, while the the women remained weak.[26] And while the most positively portrayed people in the news were indeed women, they weren't the women who were speaking out against their own abuse. They were public figures who had either reported on the #MeToo movement, founded it, or lent their support to it: Kara Swisher, Tarana Burke, Meghan Markle, Frances McDormand, and Oprah Winfrey were the top five (in that order).[27]

"The goal of the movement is to empower women," the lead researcher, Yulia Tsvetkov, said about #MeToo. "But according to our computational analysis, that's not what's happening in news stories."[28]

In our efforts to sympathize with the accusers—to ensure that women are finally listened to and not shamed or shunned—it matters that they have been so broadly depicted as lacking personal agency and power. The perception of a woman's inherent weakness, regardless of any amount of sympathy, is the psychological fodder for victim blaming. Her abuse becomes the natural consequence of her own frailty—the best she could muster in a world of male dominance and desire. This is what even the most sympathetic of #MeToo tweets can share with Chappelle's misogynistic ridicule.

Our dispositional inferences serve to buttress our Western world as it is, which is more than individualistic. It's also patriarchal. And just as easily as we fall back on negative assumptions about a woman's character in order to explain her behavior, we fall back on positive assumptions about a man's character in order to explain his—even when the behavior in question is abhorrent. Male entitlement feeds on our dispositional inferences, shape-shifting to whatever narrative it needs for justification.

When researchers at the University of Texas at Austin and Dalhousie University in Halifax, Nova Scotia, attempted to answer why sexual harassment persists—not why it happens, but why it *keeps* happening—a major reason cited was the ability of male perpetrators to create and control the narrative of who they were and why their behavior should be tolerated: "Perpetrators' ability to build myths and manipulate, shape and control information shrouded their pathologies and negative characteristics so they could harass with impunity." This was the case no matter the character they presented—be they a star who built myths about his own indispensability or a fun-loving colleague who presented his abusive behavior as harmless play.[29]

Again, this kind of a pass or benefit of the doubt is not something we extend in equal measures to the character of women. Studies show that when we see a woman yelling at a bank teller, we peg her as an overly emotional person, whereas when we see a man doing the same, we assume he's having a bad day.[30] But let's take the example of anger further, as rage and destruction are so often chalked up as the byproduct of male creative genius, serving to valorize abusive men. Consider the 2015 video interview for GQ magazine with celebrity chef David Chang, who was asked, much to his delight, about "Korean termites"—the euphemism his colleagues used to describe the damage he inflicted during his destructive rages at work. "For a while, when I was younger, opening up restaurants, I would punch walls. Or just destroy things, like a desk—a *metal* desk," he said, pausing to laugh. "It sounds childish and stupid now, but the reality is I didn't know how to express myself . . . I'm trying to take a much more enlightened approach, but it's hard—sometimes I want to punch that wall!"[31] He laughed again, as did the interviewer.

Chang's rage problem only serves to make him more real, his greatness more undeniable. If we want an explanation for his violence, it's because his character is that of a once-in-our-lifetime restaurant pioneer and perfectionist! He is *willing* his vision into reality by whatever artistic means is necessary. Moreover, he certainly isn't mangling metal furniture because he's weak or lacks agency. We would never dare ask, *Bitch, you don't know how to take a breather? Go for a fucking walk?*

Hannah Selinger, who worked as a corporate beverage director for Chang's restaurant empire in 2008, has written about being both a target and a witness of his sadistic impulses—moments that included watching Chang scream at a line chef, "I will scalp you! I will murder your fucking family!" Selinger believes Chang has avoided any true accountability for his professional misconduct precisely because he has always crafted his narrative to account for his violent temper and abusive behavior. According to her, "Part of Chang's savvy has been the mindful integration of his flaws in public; he has catalogued them throughout his career, so that the man and the myth are nearly inseparable."[32]

In his 2020 memoir *Eat a Peach*, conveniently published at a time of great reflection and reckoning about what kind of behavior we should condone in our workplaces, Chang does not shy away from his explosive temper—something for which he expresses remorse. He writes about a night at Momofuku Seiobo, in Sydney, Australia, when he stormed toward a maintenance worker in the restaurant who was whistling in a way that he found disruptive. Chang claims to have been out of his mind and struggles to recall the details. "My staff tells me I screamed at the man. Threatened him. They said I had been slicing something on a cutting board and was now gesticulating wildly with the knife. They said it could easily have been interpreted as a weapon." Chang acknowledges his compunction, adding, "I wrote an apology, but I didn't really mean it but I didn't truly know how to apologize."[33]

I wholeheartedly believe that the world stands to benefit from more men openly reflecting on their imperfections, mistakes, and low points—ideally to effect positive social change. So I commend Chang for such disclosure. And if his book's blurbs are any indication, I'm in good company. The popular organizational psychologist Adam Grant writes about Chang: "He's one of the most audaciously openhearted and honest humans you'll ever find," add-ing, "This book is for anyone who has ever felt like an underdog or an underachiever—or aspired to become an entrepreneur or a more decent person." As late-night host Jimmy Kimmel writes: "Herein you will find the recipe for one of our brightest, most energetic, talented, and inspiring Americans (who also happens to be a chef). David Chang is a great storyteller with a great story to tell."[34]

The problem, of course, is that his story is an exclusively male narrative. Think how unimaginable it would be for a woman of equal public stature to be celebrated, much less even respected, after openly acknowledging that she lost her shit while wielding a knife at someone whose whistling annoyed her. Male entitlement comes in the form of narrative license. It's the confidence and faith we place in the character of men that we're simply unwilling to grant women.

Free Will, Supersized

In 1989, not long after she moved to New York City as a graduate student, German architect and artist Karin Bruckner took a job at the firm of the famed architect Richard Meier. She would soon find herself alone with him in the office supply room. It was a Sunday afternoon and, as first reported in the *New York Times*, she was making photocopies when Meier lumbered into the room, pressed his body into hers, and began rubbing himself up and down.[35] She initially froze, processing the fact that such an eminent genius of architecture was conducting himself according to the mores of a dog park. Once the moment was over, however, Bruckner went straight to one of the firm's senior associates and told him exactly what had happened. She found his response that night, along with the responses of others with whom she shared the incident during her time at the firm, far too indifferent. "It was like, 'Yeah, this happens, but we're not going to talk about it.' It really rubbed me the wrong way—so to speak," Bruckner told me.

Germany also had its share of workplace misconduct and powerful, misbehaving men, but she felt that these things played out differently in the United States, where nobody could be inconvenienced. Her colleagues were busy working hard, proving themselves, advancing their careers, and deriving validation through their proximity to Meier's legendary status. As Bruckner explained, "Here in America, we are so focused on the individual—and their capacity and achievement—that we're not comfortable thinking critically about the well-being of others." She described a cultural force at play that's difficult to disrupt. "You know how an American refrigerator is so much bigger than a European fridge?" she asked. "The same applied to the whole phenomenon of what was happening [at the office]. Everything in this country is so supersized."

I knew exactly what she meant. I've now spent more than ten years living and working in western Europe, in very white, patriarchal societies where the misogyny and discrimination can be as bad as ours, if not worse. But I believe that there's something uniquely pernicious about how we in the United States experience workplace cruelty, and it concerns our own supersized notions of individualism and free will. We're so awash in narratives about our own potential accomplishments and success, that our own protagonism can get the best of us. Our idealized sense of self overshadows the reality of our behavior as well as the injustice that surrounds us. People everywhere tend to inflate their own abilities and morality. But the manner and magnitude of American self-aggrandizement not only sets us apart; it sets us up for a particularly acute brand of shame when we fail to live up to our ideal self.

Relative to our counterparts elsewhere, Americans are more individualistic, idealistic, and inclined to believe in heroism and personal destinies. A 2014 Pew Research Center survey of people in forty-four countries revealed Americans were outliers for their optimism and confidence in their own self-determination. More than any other nation, we place faith in hard work and its ability to pay off.[36] Earlier data on twenty-seven countries compiled by the Brookings Institution showed us believing the most devoutly that "people are rewarded for intelligence and skill."[37] According to a World Values Survey, we're also much more judgmental of the poor than our European counterparts: 60 percent of Americans believed that the poor are lazy; 26 percent of Europeans believed the same. Conversely, 60 percent of Europeans believed that the poor are trapped in poverty, while 29 percent of Americans believed the same.[38]

Our national psyche has been molded by the American Dream and its foundational faith in free will, all of which presupposes that the world is a just place. Add to this the fact that we swathe ourselves in a cultural fabric threaded with our own inherent goodness—as is certainly the case with many among my own non-immigrant, white, Christian demographic. White supremacy likes to masquerade as American exceptionalism, a belief in our nation's divine superiority. And regardless of race, a conviction in one's own specialness comes with undeniable upsides.

Dan McAdams is an author and psychologist who studies life stories, which are the narratives that we create and internalize about ourselves in order to give our lives greater coherence and purpose. Twenty-some years ago, at a conference in the Netherlands, McAdams was presenting a decade's worth of research into how life stories that emphasize suffering, redemption, and personal destiny can improve our well-being. He explained how they help us maintain hope and persevere during difficult times. Upon conclusion, the first comment came from a Dutch woman in the front row: "Professor McAdams, this is very interesting, but these life stories you describe, they seem so, well, *American*. We Europeans admire this kind of story, but it is not ours."[39]

McAdams, who reports lamely attempting to disagree with the woman, would five years later publish a book arguing her point—more specifically, that Americans are uniquely empowered by the creation of life stories that turn personal suffering into something positive; stories in which it all works out, with lessons learned and legacies left behind; stories that incorporate intrinsic virtue, inner truth, and a belief in one's own exceptionalism. Beyond their psychological and moral appeal, such stories can inspire a commitment to family, society, and future generations. And yet, for all their benefit, McAdams warns that there is also a dark side to these American life stories. "Is it not arrogant," he asks, "to imagine one's life as the full manifestation of an inner destiny? . . . Might it be an affront to those who have suffered the greatest calamities and heartaches to expect, even to suggest, that things will work out nice and happy in the end?"[40]

It doesn't help that happy endings are inescapable in America. We're incessantly subjected to them by our own media and entertainment industry—the world's largest, most profitable, and influential. "Hollywood's not called a 'dream factory' for nothing," says the American film critic Bob Mondello. "It manufactures optimism, and in the process of selling it, can make the possibility of success feel wondrously real."[41] Our imaginations are amplified by a cultural proximity to entertainment that people in most nations simply don't have. If you're a white, straight, cisgender American, you've never had a shortage of inspiration when it comes to crafting your own heroism—inspiration, importantly, served in your native language and culture. To see a fictional representation of yourself is to witness your own significance in the world. To see it day after day throughout your life is to internalize that significance—and everything it makes possible—as absolute.

In the late 1960s, while studying the sociological impact of violence on American television, the University of Pennsylvania professor George Gerbner introduced what's known as the "cultivation theory," in which he posited that long-term exposure to television programming influenced a viewer's perception of their social reality to align with the narrative message of what they were watching. The more crime Americans saw on the screen, for example, the more crime-ridden they believed their world to be. Over time, Gerbner would refine his theory to account for data indicating that the more media representations resonated with a person's immediate world, the stronger the cultivation effect would be.[42] While his arguments are not without their critics, the idea that what we see on-screen plays an important role in our social perceptions and personal attitudes has stood the test of time.[43] But perhaps more compelling, among the strongest critiques of Gerbner's hypothesis is the extent to which studies into the cultivation effect have failed to produce the same results either abroad or among foreign audiences within the United States. As an Icelandic professor of mass communications wrote about her own research on the matter: "What may be true in America is not true for the rest of the world."[44]

Ten years after Gerbner first introduced his theory, he would address a conference of U.S. television network executives concerning his increasing alarm about the depiction of sex on television and its potentially damaging impact on what he described as "the norms of basic human relationships." Despite women's recent societal advancements and their increased visibility on-screen, television stories themselves had not changed: they were failing to call out the real-world cruelty of gender dynamics, all the while increasing their depictions of sex and sexual violence. Gerbner suggested that television instilled in many of its viewers a resistance to social change as it concerned gender relations. He cited research indicating that the more television people watched, even when accounting for differences between light and heavy viewers, the more sexist were their beliefs. "Television is becoming more sexy but not less sexist," he explained. "It sets a norm that is or becomes acceptable to most, and it brings other viewers up or down to that level."[45]

Gerbner was speaking in 1980, at a time when the amount of sex and misogyny in our popular culture was about to surge. In the decades that followed, American entertainment would generate ever more hypermasculine and hyperfeminine ideals to shape our sense of social reality. Richard Goldstein, former editor of the *Village Voice*, went so far as to describe our nation's rush to invade Iraq as a political consequence of the macho, anti-feminist narrative that had come to permeate our arts and entertainment industry.[46] In 2003, he explained it to a Norwegian journalist like this: "In the United States entertainment is an immensely important means of assessing social identities. [They] appear first in culture, in a vital, sexualized form. When people subsequently adopt them, 'buy' them, they tend to become social norms. That is one of the keys to understanding the way America has evolved; cultural images become concrete models for the nation's politics. They are not fantasies, as you Europeans sometimes tend to believe, they are veritably remodeled as political and social truths."[47]

To be fair, Europeans are of course not without their own

illusions or sense of superiority. In fact, relative to our East Asian counterparts, *all* of us in the West are more likely to self-enhance—to consider our morality, abilities, and personal appeal above average. Doing so is known to boost our mental and emotional well-being in a competitive world, and has long been identified by social psychologists as directly correlated to a society's belief in individualism.[48] The more individualistic is one's culture, the logic goes, the more likely they are to self-enhance. Extensive research has revealed, however, that a much stronger predictor of a society's level of self-enhancement is their level of economic inequality. In a 2011 study conducted across five continents and fifteen countries, researchers found that the more extreme the inequality in a given society, the more inflated were its egos.[49] Here again, Americans are outliers. Those of us in the United States, along with our peers in Peru and South Africa, were significantly more likely to believe in our own superiority than those in Belgium, Germany, and Japan—three capitalist countries with remarkably lower income inequality.

I happen to now live in Belgium, where a good Walloon friend of mine recently started a business selling niche beauty products that are more popular in America than among women in this part of Europe. Having attended industry events and media training with Americans, she is frequently confused, if not amused, by their confidence. What was up, she asked me, with the constant use of "badass"? Were we really always this positive? Why the need to prove that we're such happy people? When I explained to her the particularly American practice of personal branding, she asked me, earnestly: "But for whom do they do that? Themselves?"

When the researchers linked economic inequality with self-enhancement, they theorized that the greater sense of competition found in unequal societies had motivated its citizens to believe in their own superiority. It's more comforting to think that we're somehow not as susceptible to loss or suffering than to recognize that we're one medical emergency away from needing a GoFundMe campaign to scrape by.

Essential to understand about our supersized sense of self is that it's been shaped not only by our economic inequality but by the remarkable trajectory of it. When fiscal policies introduced in the 1980s reduced taxes, deregulated markets, and cut social spending, our income inequality began a rapid escalation. In 1980 the top 1 percent of earners in the United States had 11 percent of our national income. Thirty-five years later, it had nearly doubled, to 20 percent. And while inequality rose globally, it was not nearly as drastic elsewhere as in the United States—and certainly not in western Europe, where during that same time frame the top 1 percent went from 10 to 12 percent of national income.[50] America's top 1 percent now earn an average of $1.3 million a year, three times what they made in the 1980s, while wages have remained stagnant for the bottom 50 percent of earners.[51] Today, America's top 1 percent holds more wealth than our middle class in its entirety.[52]

Such was the brunt of the neoliberal reforms touted by Ronald Reagan and the UK's Margaret Thatcher, which took our faith in free will and made it economic policy. We bought into the idea that governments don't work, markets do, and that competition would ensure we all get what's justified.[53] Taxes were slashed, social welfare spending cut, government minimized, public services privatized, and the corporate sector given free rein. Economic inequality was thus recast as the natural, moral order.[54] The United States had always been a capitalist country with a strong culture of individualism and personal responsibility, but with neoliberalism our national narrative became one of winners and losers—and it was a narrative that we deeply internalized.[55] As Thatcher herself explained to the *Sunday Times*: "Economics are the method; the object is to change the heart and soul."[56]

And change we did. It's impossible to exaggerate the political and cultural influence of forty-plus years of the neoliberal experiment. Yet rarely does it get the credit it deserves for making competition and hustle such a defining aspect of our lives. The author and environmental activist George Monbiot likens it to the people of the Soviet Union having never heard of communism.[57] Recent years have seen an increased scholarly interest in the social psychological impacts of neoliberalism, with new research linking it to ailments that include social disconnection, loneliness, violence, narcissism, and obesity.[58] The growing consensus is that our free-market economic policies, and the rationales we've internalized in order to coexist with them, if not survive them, have come to exacerbate our physical, mental, and emotional precarity.

The logic of neoliberalism is suffused throughout our media and entertainment, most unmistakably in the last twenty-five years of reality television programming.[59] Enterprising individuals engaged in zero-sum battles rife with personal humiliation mirror our larger social, economic, and political reality. Tragically, the metaphor carries over to what our children watch. When researchers at UCLA examined the values inherent to adolescent television programming over a fifty-year period in the United States, from 1967 to 2007, they found that the mid-'90s was when a seismic shift began. Prior to this point, the most prominent value in our programming was community and family. By 2007 the number one value was fame, after which came achievement, popularity, image, and financial success.[60]

It should not be surprising that the first Americans to grow up under neoliberalism—namely, my cohort, Generation X—turned out to be more individualistic, self-confident, materialistic, professionally ambitious, and money hungry than their boomer predecessors. This is according to data outlined by professor of psychology Jean Twenge in her latest book, *Generations*. Twenge writes that we Gen Xers believed what our culture told us, which was to "reach for the stars." She notes, however, that with regard to career objectives, two out of three of us haven't reached our professional goals. Our expectations were so high, it's been impossible to fulfill everything to which we've aspired.[61]

But if our culture told us to reach for the stars and we failed, neoliberalism told us it was our fault for not owning Virgin Galactic. It's an ideology that promotes self-blame, which we Americans are exceptionally good at. Be it a financial loss, home foreclosure, or unemployment, we register our hardships in particularly personal terms, whereas our peers in other countries are much more likely to fault the broader system at play.[62] And when we fall short of glory—when we end up ordinary or just plain fail—all our American supersizing sets us up for a searing disappointment in ourselves. The shame shuts us down, and the larger context of cruelty and injustice goes unchallenged.

Recent research reconsiders how we experience shame by contrasting it to our experiences with guilt. Whereas guilt implies the failure to live up to the standards of our moral self, shame isn't actually concerned with moral worth. Rather, shame is the perceived discrepancy between who we are and who we had hoped to be.

"What matters to the ashamed person is *not* his or her responsibility for the fault," researchers write, "but how this fault impacts on his or her ideal self."[63]

When I blamed myself for what had happened with Charlie, that was more than a patriarchal narrative; it was also a deeply American one. I went into the working world believing in my own invincibility. Instead, I became side entertainment for a boss with palsied hands. The sensation of failure and self-disgust was crippling. In a world of limitless personal potential, I had no vocabulary for the disappointment.

CHAPTER TWO

The Harm in Harmonizing

Charlie brought a young woman into the office one April morning and dumped her among the open-floor plan like a box that needed storage. Nobody on staff had been informed about her or the arrival of anyone new. She had relocated to New York City from Idaho, where Charlie had met her on a recent work trip and extended a job offer. She was one of a few people during my year and a half at the show, all of whom were women, who were brought on both unexpectedly and without a job title. I may not have known what exactly led to their hire, but I felt that I knew these women's struggles, more specifically the discomfort that comes with sensing your employment is based on something other than merit. You try your hardest to prove otherwise, which is all but impossible for those whose professional responsibilities haven't actually been specified.

I like to think I was kind to other women starting out at the show, but the truth of my track record includes some monstrous moments. This particular new hire was a disconcertingly waifish blonde. I would watch her self-consciously pass the time, struggling to purpose herself in the absence of any work. She moved softly, sat rigidly, and had a baldish spot on the crown of her head. Occasionally, she would reach up with a bone-thin hand and adjust her hair so as to conceal her scalp. I wanted to give her a gentle hug and tell her that none of us felt confident about our places, either.

And then one day I heard a fellow producer call her Kojak, and I laughed out loud.

"Hey, where's Kojak?" he asked while registering her absence that morning. It didn't matter that I had little familiarity with the 1970s New York detective series starring a bald Telly Savalas; I found it funny. In my memory, what came out of me was a brief, loud bleat—the kind of sudden, pressured laugh that has a note of shock and mischief in it. The kind of laugh one makes when they know *very* well that they shouldn't be laughing.

I am keenly aware of how horrible this was. I have close friends who have struggled all their lives with anorexia. I know that eating disorders are as deadly as they are stigmatized, misunderstood, and difficult to overcome. More hypocritically, on a few occasions in college, I myself downed laxatives after eating what I considered a damning quantity of late-night cheesesteaks—which qualified me, at the very least, as a disordered eater. Yet I had laughed at the signs of starvation in one of my peers. I had even forgotten about this cruel joke and my own unempathetic encouragement until revisiting the past with former colleagues, so many of whom talked about how much they had appreciated the humor in the office, and how some on staff could make us laugh in the darkest of times. Their humor had created a profound sense of belonging that made our jobs manageable—sometimes even enjoyable. But it had also helped normalize an abusive workplace.

The producer who made the Kojak joke would later support the women who spoke out against Charlie. He's a vegetarian with a deep concern about animal cruelty, someone who, I am told, put his life on hold for more than a year to help care for his dying uncle. Six years after I left the show, having not seen or talked to him during that time, I agreed to a first date with my now husband because I saw on social media that he and this producer were friends. As horrified as I am that I laughed at another woman's suffering, I'm equally as aghast by whom I laughed about it with. But sadistic jokes were possible precisely because we believed we were in the company of good, well-intentioned people. We could joke that way because we *knew* we knew better.

No kind of laugh makes us feel more connected than one we know we shouldn't be enjoying. It's a shared transgression that leaves us feeling fortunate to have been included. The same can go for a work environment that, on some level, we know we shouldn't be condoning. The inappropriateness, even the cruelty, can create a powerful sense of connection and loyalty that overrides our moral judgment. Our understanding and appreciation of what's appropriate professional conduct can change with the times, but one thing will always remain the same: our desire to get along with others.

We harmonize in groups, adapting ourselves to one another and our shared circumstances, and according to what can make us feel competent and liked by our peers. It's what human evolution has conditioned us to do—and we do it spectacularly well in the context of our workplace hierarchies. In ways we're conscious of and in many ways that we're not, our behavior is profoundly impacted by the people who surround us.

The Need to Belong

A woman named Molly told me that her dream of someday working for CBS's *60 Minutes* began when she was ten years old, on the day she and her parents met with two of the show's news producers. They had traveled from Nashville to the network's Manhattan headquarters to share Molly's story of being abused at a children's center. More than a dozen other families were now alleging the similar treatment of their own children, as it was becoming increasingly evident that administrators had turned a blind eye to some shockingly horrific behavior. The news story never came to fruition, but Molly was powerfully impacted by the idea that investigative journalism could be a voice for those who needed it. During her senior year of college in New York City, she would get her foot in the door as one of the show's interns. Two years and an enormous amount of unpaid labor later, Molly was hired as a broadcast associate for *60 Minutes*.

She was there to work and to work hard, and in the process she put functionality over style. She'd wear pants and comfortable shoes, which stood out from the chicer sartorial standards upheld by other women on staff. Socializing with colleagues also never felt as pressing for Molly as the job she wanted to be doing. Gradually, however, she realized that something was awry with her place in the office. Sometimes she felt a little frumpy, but other times she felt invisible. "I just didn't feel like I fit in," she told me over a Zoom call. "It was the same feeling I had in middle school, where all the cool kids are over here and I'm like this tomboy who can't register on their radar."

It was almost a year into her job when two senior-level female employees pulled Molly aside with a warning that had nothing to do with the quality of her work. "People find you unapproachable," they told her. They were light on details but informed her that she had one month to turn things around.

"I went home and was like, *What can I do to change this?*" she recalled. "The next day I showed up in a dress and heels. That breaks my heart looking back." She stayed for about a week before realizing there was no way to remedy the situation short of pretending to be somebody who she wasn't. So she quit.

A former CBS colleague with whom Molly worked closely had left the network to work for another investigative news series and was quick to extend a job offer in the hope that she would join him. She was grateful for the opportunity, and she took it. But she wasn't spared from something deeply scarring. "What infuriates me are the long-lasting effects of this," she said. "I've spent the last eight years struggling to find something else that I care about in the same way, because I've just been so terrified and insecure. Am I good? Am I a fraud? It destroyed me."

This kind of personal devastation makes sense from an evolutionary perspective when we consider that the relatively safe, bureaucratic workplaces of today are a mere blip on the time line of human history. The vast majority of our existence as a species has been spent hunting and gathering in circumstances where our lives depended upon being a welcomed member of a tribe. In fact, our predecessors' ability to live as members of a group—to cooperate and maintain harmonious relationships—may have been the most important predictor of their survival.[1] To be disliked by one's peers could mean ostracization or death.[2] Today, how we're perceived by others still remains one of our strongest preoccupations as humans.

"Everyone, no exception, must have a tribe," wrote the sociobiologist E. O. Wilson. "In ancient history and prehistory, tribes gave visceral comfort and pride from familiar fellowship, and a way to defend the group enthusiastically against rival groups. It gave people a name in addition to their own and social meaning in a chaotic world . . . Human nature has not changed."[3] This reality was apparent when I spoke with people who had failed to bond with their colleagues or who had never been welcomed by an in-group at work, experiences that had painfully chomped away at their sense of worth. As with Molly, it had haunted some of them for years—even, and sometimes especially, when they had rationally concluded that the tribe in question was not where they would ever want to belong.

What's most insidious about the pain of social rejection is that it's not rational; it's instinctual. Studies show that when we experience a social threat, such as exclusion, the same neural circuitry that causes us to feel physical harm is activated in our brain. "Just as physical pain has evolved to alert us that 'something has gone wrong' with our bodies, social pain is a similarly potent signal that alerts us when 'something has gone wrong' with our social connections to others, an equally important threat to the survival of our species," write the UCLA psychologists Naomi Eisenberger and Matthew Lieberman.[4] Such neural wiring is why Tylenol proves capable of also alleviating emotional pain.[5]

In his book *Social: Why Our Brains Are Wired to Connect*, Lieberman explains that, neurologically speaking, we have two distinct networks, one for social thinking and one for nonsocial thinking. His research shows that our brain's default mode, or resting state, is with the social network activated and that whenever we finish any kind of nonsocial thinking—e.g., loading the dishwasher, paying bills, or doing that day's daily crossword—our social wiring reflexively turns back on. As Lieberman told *Scientific American*: "Evolution has placed a bet that the best thing for our brain to do in any spare moment is to get ready to see the world socially."[6]

This irrepressible drive for social connection is evidenced by the extent to which we mimic those around us. People like us more when we behave like them, so we unconsciously mirror their gestures and expressions, even assume their linguistical quirks as our own. Scientists describe this mimicry as social glue, and its impact on our emotional disposition is significant.[7] For instance, when we mimic somebody's smile, our brains can register our dilated pupils and contracting facial muscles *before* processing the corresponding emotion of happiness—meaning that our physiology is capable of dictating our feelings. It also means that when we smooth out our facial muscles by paralyzing them with injections of Botox, fMRI scans of our brains reveal that we end up *feeling* less.[8] I don't share this to make women my age question their dermatological choices but to underscore how involuntary, instantaneous, and powerful our responsiveness can be to others. We are each endowed with an element of evolutionary biology that doesn't give a shit about professionalism or politics; it wants only to increase our ability to belong, and that has real implications when it comes to the dynamics we create in the workplace.

When I first began working for Charlie, I was frequently annoyed with how giddily I smiled at him. As a man of extremes, when he was in a good mood, he was *ecstatic*, and I would beam back with equal exuberance. The importance of smiling is culturally instilled in women, but this was something more—like an uncontrollable receptiveness that I couldn't muffle. I was never actually feeling joy in these moments, only relief that he was in his happy place and not his angry one. But I hated myself for failing to project something more subdued, more professional. How hard could that be?

What I didn't know at the time was how difficult it is *not* to return a smile—that people tend to beam back all the more if they are of a lower status, and that women are more susceptible to emotional contagion than men.[9] Moreover, all this constant, uncontrollable adapting of our behavior to resonate with those in our midst is a normal aspect of mental and emotional health. Part of the struggle for individuals with autism is that such mimicry doesn't come naturally to them.[10] Those who are neurotypical give no thought to revising themselves according to whether they're with colleagues as opposed to friends as opposed to intimate partners and so on. Who we are in every moment is variable, redetermined constantly by those who surround us.

Many Americans, of course, spend more hours a week in the physical presence of their colleagues than they do anyone else, including their families. According to data published by the American Time Use Survey in 2020, this is especially true for young adults in their twenties, who as they then go through their thirties and forties still spend roughly as much time with their coworkers as they do their partners.[11] We don't yet have reliable insight into how the emergence of hybrid work is changing things beyond knowing that more of us are spending greater amounts of time at home and assumably with family. There's no doubt, though, that even in a post-pandemic world our colleagues maintain enormous influence over our day-to-day disposition. And in our sedentary, technological age of computer monitors, email, and Slack channels—all of which bucks what human evolution has prescribed for our own well-being—our coworkers are a lifeline. Something meaningful and sustaining is created. It may not always be principled or benevolent or inclusive, but it's meaningful for many people nonetheless. Bonding with colleagues—be it through jokes, office gossip, shared anxiety, or sheer exhaustion—is the "visceral comfort" of which E. O. Wilson wrote about our tribes.

It also turns out that the more adverse, insane, indeed abusive our workplaces, the more significant and stronger our bonding can be. Our social glue becomes a social superglue. A 2014 study led by researchers at both the University of New South Wales and the University of Queensland revealed the extent to which individuals who together experienced pain—actual, physical pain—also experienced positive social cohesion and solidarity. Participants in small groups were randomly assigned work that was either painful or relatively painless. For example, one group performed a task with their forearms submerged in water that was excruciatingly cold, while the other group did so in water that was room temperature. One group had to work while enduring a brutal wall squat, while the other group could stand on only one foot at a time. When participants were later asked to rate statements about how they felt toward the group, those who had experienced pain indicated a greater level of bonding with their peers. More compelling still, these individuals also went on to show increased cooperation at additional tasks as well as a greater willingness to put the well-being of the group ahead of their own personal outcomes.[12]

Whether the shared pain is physical or emotional in its nature, group bonding ensues. This was certainly evident among Charlie's staff, many of whom spoke of their colleagues from that time as singularly special. "He was a maniacal asshole who took years off my life," said a former producer who still has nightmares about him. But she would do it all over again, she told me, because of the people she'd gotten to know "in the trenches." There was no shortage of war references in my conversations with former colleagues. "It was trench warfare, and we were all in the trenches together," a former male producer said. "In fact, it was just like what people say about war: I never formed such a bond and had as much fun except for the bit where someone was shooting at me." That so many of us relied on war metaphors to describe working for Charlie is, at best, linguistically lazy. At worst, it's highly insensitive to anyone who's actually been in combat. But there's an important admission in these analogies, which is that working for Charlie was the closest thing to war that most of us had experienced.

Groupthink thrives in this kind of a warped, white-collar "war zone" in part because the rewards can feel so, so good. In the words of my three-year-old son's favorite song, from *The Lego Ninjago Movie* soundtrack: "What a ride / I knew I was strong / Now I found my place / . . . I'm where I belong . . ." Our shared struggle and perseverance give us meaning and a sense of accomplishment that's beyond what we've felt in other, more humane and mundane work environments. The extreme highs and lows that play off each other are addictive. Like the physically ailing distance runner who can't stop running marathons, some people described working for hostile bosses as something they couldn't quit. "There has to be a neurological component to it, right?" asked a woman who had worked in radio. "Like it's a drug, and you get your hits, and they become your supply."

In his book *Tribe: On Homecoming and Belonging*, Sebastian Junger explores the psychological impact of modern life's ease and safety. We're missing out, he says, on the hardships that have historically provided a sense of meaning and community. He cites multiple studies showing that war can positively impact mental health by reinforcing social bonds and collective purpose. "Adversity often leads people to depend more on one another, and that closeness can produce a kind of nostalgia for the hard times that even civilians are susceptible to," he writes. He quotes a Londoner who, in the aftermath of World War II, professed to miss the perilousness of the Blitz: "I wouldn't mind having an evening like it, say, once a week—ordinarily there's no excitement." A survivor of the AIDS epidemic acknowledged longing for the human connectedness of the '80s: "I must admit that I miss those days of extreme brotherhood . . . which led to deep emotions and understandings that are above anything I have felt since the plague years."[13]

Working for an abusive boss was the closest that my colleagues and I could get to the exhilaration and kinship of the trenches. Affluence these days often begets isolation, depression, and a loss of community. A group high on trust funds and Ivy League degrees can be drawn to a boss like Charlie not in spite of his nastiness but precisely *because* of it—and the struggle it creates. And once they find their place in this tribe, it would feel dishonorable to question or confront its chief. A male producer from before my time was emphatic that nobody in the office considered Charlie's treatment of staff to be okay. Rather, they assumed it was the sacrifice necessary to be a part of something important. "Think about all the good people who worked on that show," he told me. "And how smart they were and informed about the world, and how not a single one of them, at least when I was there, indicated ever wanting to do anything about it."

"A Soldier Does Not Ask Whether It Is Good or Bad"

In May 2007, a manager at a motivational sales firm in Utah asked his employees to break for a team-building exercise intended to address their lagging sales numbers. He marched them outside and up an incline, then asked for a volunteer. Not knowing what he was agreeing to but wanting to prove his loyalty and determination, an employee name Chad stepped forward.

The manager had Chad lie on the ground with his head facing downhill. He then asked his colleagues to hold Chad's arms and legs in place as he slowly poured a gallon jug of water over his mouth and nostrils. Chad, thinking he was going to die, thrashed his arms and legs while attempting to escape. But he was no match for his peers, who continued, as instructed, to hold him down until their manager was finished with the form of torture known as waterboarding.

"You saw how hard Chad fought for air right there," the manager addressed his team. "I want you to go back inside and fight that hard to make sales."[14] And allegedly that was that. The physical torture of their colleague was water under the bridge as they returned to their work making sales calls on behalf of Trump University.

While Chad's colleagues likely had no prior experience with waterboarding, we can assume that they knew he was struggling to breathe and that he desperately wanted to be released. That they allowed the torture to continue speaks to the extreme to which we do what's expected of us. Professional success most often demands heeding authority and going along with established norms. Especially in hierarchical workplaces, we harmonize because nobody wants to make things harder or more complicated than necessary for their group. Expectations are also straightforward, whereas, by comparison, pushing back is muddled by uncertainty and fears of tribal exclusion.

When Stanley Milgram conducted his notorious shock experiment in the early 1960s, he wanted to know how obedient subjects would be when it required hurting another human. Milgram's "authority" was a mannerly scientist in a lab coat who asked forty men between the ages of twenty and fifty to administer electric shocks to a stranger. Seated in front of an electric shock generator with a line of switches that ranged from an uncomfortable 15 volts (labeled "SLIGHT SHOCK") to a potentially lethal 450 volts ("DANGER: SEVERE SHOCK"), the participants were instructed to give a word-pairing test to a man whose nearby body was strapped down and attached to the generator by electrodes. This man was an actor collaborating with Milgram, but participants believed him to be a fellow volunteer to whom they were asked to administer a shock each time he failed to provide the right answer. With each additional wrong response, the electric shock that the men were asked to deliver had progressively more voltage and received louder expressions of pain and protest in return. Importantly, participants were told they could stop at any time without forfeiting the agreed-upon payment of four dollars.

Prior to conducting his study, Milgram polled his academic peers and psychiatrists for their predictions. They guessed that most would refuse or certainly wouldn't go past the point at which the actor cried out to be released. Only "a pathological fringe" of 1 or 2 percent was expected to reach the highest voltage.[15] In the end, 65 percent of the participants issued the maximum shock to an individual screaming in pain from the next room.

In the decades since, various replications and iterations of Milgram's experiment have all produced the same general outcome—even as his original methodology has faced criticism.* Psychologists have moved away from questioning the results to begin instead

---

*   Most notably, Milgram has been criticized for bullying his study's participants, and for the fact that many of them later reported knowing that the shocks they had administered were fake.

rethinking what they actually mean. Are we really so spinelessly obedient? Is there really that much cruelty inside us, waiting for the right circumstances to manifest itself?[16] Many, including the Dutch historian Rutger Bregman, have concluded that the study's results are better understood in terms of a human desire to be helpful, as participants trusted the experimenter and many of them believed that they were contributing to important research. In his book *Humankind: A Hopeful History*, Bregman quotes a psychologist who, after repeating Milgram's experiments, emphasized that, "People go to great lengths, will suffer great distress, to be good . . ."[17]

Bregman's take resonates with one of Milgram's own conclusions, which was that when someone is in a subservient position to an authority, their thinking is consumed by a sense of duty to the relationship. When inflicting the painful shocks, the men had not lost their moral sense but had instead *redirected* it toward successfully doing what was expected of them. He wrote: "In wartime, a soldier does not ask whether it is good or bad to bomb a hamlet; he does not experience shame or guilt in the destruction of a village: rather he feels pride or shame depending on how well he has performed the mission assigned to him."[18]

In our individualistic society, where weakness is despised and work defines so much of our identity, being good at our jobs implies an integrity of its own regardless of the work at hand. This truth is captured powerfully by the filmmaker Kitty Green in her movie *The Assistant*. Based on reported events at the Weinstein Company and reflective of some one hundred interviews that Green conducted with former assistants in the film and other industries, the movie depicts the mundane dutifulness and psychological perseverance required to work for an omnipotent, unhinged abuser. The assistant, played by Julia Garner, is the first one in the office predawn and among the last to leave late at night. Mixed with her numerous administrative tasks and phone responsibilities, she cleans the stains off her boss's office sofa and properly disposes of his used syringes. Although her awareness of events lacks specifics, she is, categorically, complicit in her boss's behavior. And yet the viewer will find her anything if not good. As the personification of an excellent employee, she maintains a certain virtuousness, even within the context of an industry rape mill.

The movie also illustrates how hard it can be to go against expectations from above when Garner tries to report her boss and is made to doubt herself by a belittling HR employee. Doing her job, and doing it well, is clear-cut. But stopping her daily routine to proactively question authority elicits discomforting uncertainty. Green said that in her interviews with assistants, "gaslit" was a word that came up a lot, particularly for those who had turned to HR: "the idea that you always leave the room kind of doubting, or being confused about why you even went in in the first place," she told a reporter, adding that the HR rep she scripted is neither angry nor cruel. Rather, he is clear in his thinking, and his logic makes sense. "She's got the dots, she just can't join them," explained Green.[19]

Most often, however, we don't need HR to convince us to stay quiet, because every other silent employee has already led by example. In fact, the more people involved in what's going on, the less likely anyone is to speak out. As a former producer lamented about Charlie's abusive berating of our staff: "It's hard to explain to people who don't understand how these things happen that when you work in a massive office where everything is on display, you wouldn't have spoken up. What could you say?"

Social psychologists call this "diffusion of responsibility": the more people present, the harder it is to know our own role and responsibility. What could we possibly do? And why us instead of somebody else? If nobody has already spoken out, why should we think there's a need to? Coupled with the ambiguity comes apprehension. Will we seem whiny? Or maybe self-righteous? "Our fear of embarrassment is the tip of the iceberg that is the ancient fear of exclusion, and it turns out to be astonishingly potent," writes the business leader and author Margaret Heffernan. "We are more likely to intervene when we are the sole witness; once there are other witnesses, we become anxious about doing the right thing (whatever that is), about being seen and being judged by the group."[20]

In her book *Willful Blindness*, Heffernan explains how diffusion of responsibility can make us bystanders to some of the most inexplicably malicious, illegal, or even deadly activity at work. She tells the story of a hospital nurse so hostile to the elderly in her care that they would avoid drinking fluids for fear of needing a bedpan. Hospital staff all knew that she was abusive and jeopardizing the health of patients, and they discussed their concerns with each other. But they wrongly interpreted their talk as action when in reality, everyone was in a holding pattern, comfortably waiting for somebody else to do something.[21] "Knowledge confers responsibility but when everyone knows, who is responsible?" writes Heffernan. "It's the easiest thing in the world to assume that it is someone else: someone smarter, more powerful, more senior, more articulate, bolder, older: anyone as long as it isn't me."[22]

In the 1968 "smoky-room experiment," subjects were asked to fill out a survey in a room that slowly began to fill with smoke. Those who were alone in the room responded quickly—tending to look for the origin of the smoke or go get help, as three-quarters of them did within the first six minutes. But when a subject was seated with two actors who seemed indifferent to the smoke, a mere 10 percent addressed the situation. A third variation of the experiment placed three actors in the room, some of whom coughed and indicated difficulty seeing but who nevertheless remained indifferent. In this scenario, only 38 percent of subjects reported the smoke.[23]

To be human is to be reluctant to go out on a limb. And young entry-level workers—those who are experiencing their first professional culture and, in some cases, their first exposure to unbridled power—are often the most reluctant. Time and again people cited their youth to explain why they had silently trudged along, regretting the extent to which they had assumed that the toxicity and abuse were simply par for the course. "You think this is how it works. It sets your blueprint for how professional life is," a colleague from *Charlie Rose* told me. He had begun working at the show long before I started, shortly after he graduated college, and told me that he still struggles to understand the multiple years he spent as a devoted employee. "There was a certain self-abnegation that everyone who worked there experienced, and even the most skillful communicator can't communicate what it's like. It's like that Lady Gaga song where she says, '*'Til it happens to you, you don't know how it feels.*'"

Emotional Labor

"You're never going to believe this," Charlie began with disdain, and I knew it was imperative that I appear overly concerned in anticipation. "You know that Fareed Zakaria is getting his own show on CNN?" I nodded attentively as he proceeded to tell me that Zakaria had called our executive producer to find out whom he could contact at Ralph Lauren so that he, like Charlie, could be provided with free suits for taping. Charlie's preference for wearing Ralph Lauren had begun some twenty years earlier when the fashion designer, himself a devoted fan of the show, began meeting Charlie's on-air sartorial needs by regularly sending free, appropriately sized suits, shirts, and ties to the office. Charlie's outrage was palpable. "Fareed thinks Ralph Lauren gives out suits to people just because they're on television! Can you believe that?"

I could *completely* believe it. In fact, to me it sounded logical. But that's not how I chose to respond to my boss, who was looking for my sympathetic indignation. I sighed with feigned disbelief and shook my head. Charlie continued: "Ralph sends me suits because I am *me* and because he's always been a big fan of what *I* do." I shook my head some more.

My boss was entitling himself to my care and attention—emotional labor that he would never have asked of any of my male colleagues. And I provided it freely. There are times when we harmonize in ways that are beyond our control, but this was different. It was both mindful and performative—and done for the sake of being exactly who the man at the top needed me to be in that moment.

In 1983, the sociologist Arlie Russell Hochschild coined the term "emotional labor" to describe the unrecognized, uncompensated work that many women and low-income workers perform "trying to feel the right feeling for the job." Think flight attendant, nurse, server, or customer service agent, who invariably have to manage the tenor of their interactions with a smile or reassuring voice. "This labor requires one to induce or suppress feeling in order to sustain the outward countenance that produces the proper state of mind in others," she wrote in her landmark book *The Managed Heart*.[24] Her concern was the toll this kind of performance took on the mental health of employees, who could become withdrawn from their daily work and out of touch with their own true feelings.

While Hochschild's research focused on service workers, white-collar female employees can also be exploited by emotional labor, particularly by male superiors hungry for assurance of their social stature and manliness.

But first, a necessary qualifier about emotional labor. In recent years, as women have examined the often invisible, disproportionate amount of labor they shoulder at home relative to their male partners, the term has become a catchall for labor that women feel emotions about.[25] That's according to Haley Swenson, who focuses on gender equality in the workplace at the think tank New America, and who cautions against using the term too broadly. "We lose the kind of specificity that can help identify what's really going on—and how power has become unequally distributed," she told me. Emotional labor, she says, comes down to this: Do you need to manage your or someone else's emotions in order to get your job done? If the answer is yes, it's emotional labor.[26]

In my own experience and that of many women, tending to the emotional state of our male bosses—be it with smiles, a sympathetic ear, or the indulging of their humor—wasn't listed in our job description, but it was expected of us nonetheless. It was a playful, sensitive, feminine kind of companionship, and a defining element of our daily drudge. It introduced itself bit by bit, increasingly pushing boundaries, making us ever more vulnerable and in some cases priming us for abuse. For an outsider, it could have seemed like innocent fun or maybe a gross brand of older-guy attention seeking. But when we look at it through the lens of emotional labor, we can illuminate more of the "specificity" Swenson mentioned within the power dynamic at play.

In former New York governor Andrew Cuomo's world, emotional labor was an institutional demand, setting up a chummy, flirtatious dynamic that, once in place, made it harder for the women in question to firmly opt out. Charlotte Bennett, who was among the first to speak out against Cuomo's conduct, was tasked with companionship from the moment she began as his executive assistant—a job that she described to state attorneys as "trying to like thread this needle of not making him angry but also maintaining . . . what I see as appropriate behavior."[27] Her first week, he asked her to memorize the lyrics to a song he later demanded they sing together. Not long after that, he invited her to work out with him. At the gym, he made jokes and inquired about both her relationship status as well as the reputation of his own hand size—what Bennett knew he meant as the rumored size of his genitalia.[28]

Cuomo also sought Bennett out in private to make her a confidante. During their first conversation alone, he asked her personal questions, and she revealed as much as she felt was expected. She told him that she was a survivor of sexual violence and that his signing of Enough is Enough, New York State's sexual assault policy for protecting college students, had changed her life for the better. The exchange was emotional. She said Cuomo had tears in his eyes while explaining how important it was for women to feel safe.[29] These moments of coerced intimacy work to undermine a woman, making her feel as though she has already ceded something of herself and her expectations that she can't win back. As multiple prior encounters with the governor likely did to Bennett, the day she was alone with him taking dictation, and he asked that she turn off the recorder so he could tell her that he was lonely; ask her if she had trouble with intimacy, given her history with sexual violence; ask her if age difference mattered to her in a relationship; and tell her, unsolicited, that he considered any woman twenty-two years or older a suitable sexual partner.

The power differential alone makes this situation fraught and complicated to manage, but by this point Bennett was five months into a work relationship that had taken on a confessional element. As she explained in a television interview, with her voice beginning to shake, she had hesitated to come forward initially because when the governor had asked her inappropriate questions, she had answered them honestly. "I think that was where I held the most shame," she said.

"Why did you feel shame?" the interviewer, CBS News's Norah O'Donnell, asked.

"I feel that people put the onus on the woman to shut that conversation down. And by answering I was somehow engaging in that, or enabling it, when in fact, I was just terrified."[30]

When norms of professionalism have already given way to something more intimate, unequivocally putting the kibosh on your boss's behavior can feel erratic—if not manic. It doesn't take a famous governor to create this kind of entrapment. It just takes enough prior boundary pushing to leave a woman feeling that she has compromised her full right to professional standards.

Still, for other women I talked to, emotional labor had spawned an elusive but undeniable companionship with their boss. A thirty-eight-year-old woman who worked for a small creative agency told me her former boss was an unmarried, seemingly lonely man in his fifties who always overshared—and expected the same of her. His detailed knowledge of her personal life could be of enormous benefit, like the time he helped her family access better medical care for her younger brother with a rare lung condition. "He had this really generous paternal side that gave me a lot of comfort, but it also meant that he was expecting us to be like family. Sometimes it was okay, but other times I'm sitting there and he's telling me about the porn he watched in the hotel on his last work trip, or he's patting me on the head like I'm his golden retriever," she said. "It's so hard to explain. He was my best and my worst boss at the same time."

We can recognize these men's inappropriateness and that we are being put upon while also seeing, as we have been conditioned to, a humanity in the situation. It might be their loneliness, insecurity, madness, or some other trait with which, like it or not, we've become intimately familiar. And which, like it or not, summons our sympathies.

The author and family therapist Terrence Real, who specializes in issues of gender and power, believes that one of the most unrecognized psychological forces in the world is a female impulse to safeguard the male sense of self. He describes it as a dynamic that can manifest in any relationship with a masculine and a feminine side to it, be it a husband and wife, a parent and a child, a hostage and a kidnapper, or any two colleagues. "Whoever inhabits the feminine side of the equation has a deep compulsion to protect the disowned fragility of whoever is on the masculine side of the equation, even while being hurt by that person," says Real. "You protect your perpetrator. You protect power."[31]

Emotional labor brings this feminine role to the fore and makes its performance more visceral than how we might normally act upon the impulse to shield a man's ego. Our abuse gets complicated by an unshakable need to protect the feelings of our abusers, regardless of how irrational and counterproductive we know this is. "I had to become comfortable with him being uncomfortable," a woman told me about finding the courage to file an HR report against a male superior. Real believes that what made the #MeToo movement so revolutionary was that it dared to go against this tendency, which he considers a core demand of the patriarchy.[32]

"I pretended like nothing was happening, and the reason why was because I felt so badly for him," Charlie's former assistant, Kyle Godfrey-Ryan, told me about the times he would inappropriately touch her when she worked for him in the mid-2000s.[33] "I really, deeply respected him as a human being and I hated watching him do these things, even if they were to me."

From day one of her job, Godfrey-Ryan felt compelled to be Charlie's friend and, even more so, his caretaker. She knew well which factors contributed to his bad behavior and, depending on his schedule and how much he'd slept, she could anticipate when she might be subjected to his rage. She worried about his loneliness, his eating habits, and the physical toll of his work. But she worried most about Charlie during the holidays, when his lack of family felt most palpable. This was when she'd set aside all the times he'd called her stupid and worthless—all the verbal abuse she claims hurt more than any of his handsiness—to call and check on him. He would receive invitations from friends in high places, she recalled, but he never accepted. "He would end up alone and then he would end up physically sick every time," she told me, still sounding sad for him.

The world needs compassion. In fact, it could use a lot more of it. But it's a problem when that compassion undermines our own self-protection and well-being. As for Godfrey-Ryan, her concern for Charlie never subsided, but nor did it get the best of her. She became the first woman to go on the record with accusations against him. The day the story was published, she and her two young children said a prayer for him. "We create something called a love bubble, where you rub your hands together and charge the energy. They each sent one out to him," she told me. Her daughter added peace to her bubble, while her son gave his lavender, for soothing. "They were so afraid that he was so old that he'd never get a second chance to do the right thing."

CHAPTER THREE

The Myth of Who
We Think We Are

One night in 2008, after a work event with Charlie, I accepted a
ride with him back uptown in his chauffeured Mercedes. Though I
don't remember the early minutes of the ride, I recall the moment,
as the car headed north on Fifth Avenue, when he grabbed the hair
at the nape of my neck and pulled my face toward him, growling
into my ear, "Tell me, huh? Tell me what you want."

Honest answers could have included a lower APR on at least one
of my credit cards, a puppy, laser hair removal—but that's not what
he wanted to know. Charlie often demanded affirmation from his staff,
fishing and prodding to extract signs of their devotion to him and his
brand. He needed to hear frequently about how badly we all wanted
to work for him. But that evening I didn't say anything. I was numb
with exhaustion, my will worn down by the sustained effort of trying
to avoid or manage moments like these. I'd been an intern at the show
for ten months and was performing the workload of a producer while
going to graduate school full-time. I was too tired to respond at all.

His grip tightened and his tone changed to something question-ably sadistic. "What do you want?" I began to think he might be inquiring about something different than my professional desires. He said it again, this time more slowly. "Tell . . . me . . . what . . . you . . . want."

What came next was not premeditated, and—given that I was always silent when he'd corner, grope, or dirty-talk me—I think we were both stunned when it came out: "I have a really small vagina."

He let go of my hair and pulled away. The remainder of the car ride was silent and ranks among my darkest moments with Charlie. I didn't know why I had just said what I said, other than that I had recently started watching Sarah Silverman's new show, which was heavy on the vagina jokes. To be clear: I have no actual knowledge about how my vagina compares, size-wise, to those of other women. The female anatomy doesn't lend itself to locker room comparisons or bragging rights, if that's even what I had done.

The reality was that I didn't think Charlie could actually have sex that easily, and certainly not with the virile stiffness required for sex with a smaller, presumably tighter vagina. He had two open-heart surgeries under his belt, and during moments of aggressive grabbing and rubbing I'd never detected even the slightest erection. Along with his despotic temperament and constant need for affir-mation, this had led me to believe that for Charlie it was far more about power than about getting off. He didn't want sex from me; he simply wanted the confirmation that he *could* dominate me in whatever way he wanted, *if* he wanted.

Riding uptown next to him in silence, I had no idea how he'd interpreted my words. As a humble offering? A jab at his manli-ness? I didn't know which was worse, especially since that week I was waiting to receive my start date as an associate producer at his show. With no other job prospects, I would soon be making the transition from living in New York City *on* student loans to living in New York City *owing* student loans—$179,000 total for both undergrad and grad school. After the driver dropped us off outside Charlie's Fifth Avenue apartment, I walked west along the dark stretch of Central Park South to take the A train home to Washington Heights. I felt utterly alone. There was nobody in my life to help me make sense of what had just happened because there was nobody with whom I could share it. I thought that everyone, even my closest friends, would think that deep down I actually wanted his advances—something I had projected onto others because I already believed some version of it myself.

More than shame, I felt *coreless*. Whoever I believed myself to be when I'd arrived at that internship, she disappeared every time I had an encounter with Charlie. And that night, after I talked about my small vagina to a skeevy older man from whom I was trying to get a job, I had never been more unrecognizable to myself.

Today, I'd like to think that I said it to flip the script: to throw Charlie's lewdness back at him and, just maybe, to make him feel like the weak one for once. That might have been the case. A far better explanation, though, concerns what psychologists interviewed for this book have explained to me, which is that to be human is to frequently be a crackpot. We live at the mercy of all kinds of cultural inputs and internal acrobatics that keep us from understanding ourselves, or even controlling ourselves, the way we think we do. None of us are as coherent or consistent as we think we are. We feel this in moments that catch us off guard or make us feel threatened, when we react in unexpectedly strange ways that don't make any sense at all. But even in normal circumstances, we unconsciously work to iron out discrepancies in our personal conduct. As the experimental psychologist Bruce Hood explains, "We effortlessly and sometimes unknowingly reinterpret our behavior to make it seem that we had deliberately made the choices all along. We are constantly telling stories to make sense of ourselves."[1]

Who we are is a story, and it's a story that we're incessantly crafting in a way that's easier to live with. We edit and reinterpret events to make ourselves a more worthy, reliable protagonist—and while it's these coherent, consistent selves who are the characters in the stories we tell about sexual misconduct, it's often our inconsistent ones who appear in the moment. Our complicity is found in the gap between the reality of our behavior and who we believe ourselves to be—and that latter person is a myth.

We Are Our Stories

We all have moments when we don't know why we said what we said. A war correspondent named Danielle told me about a U.S. military officer who made a pass at her while she was reporting in Afghanistan. Her automatic response, she recalled in disbelief, was one of gratitude. "Oh my God, thank you so much," Danielle had said to him. "I can't even believe you would be interested in me." She told him that she *wished* she could and then offered up a rambling explanation as to why exactly she couldn't that involved his wife and four children back home. "I can't risk letting you break my heart," she heard herself say. It was effective insofar as he moved on, but she was aghast by the ease of her performance and how quick she was to explain herself when he was the one behaving inappropriately.

Behind every woman's real-time encounter with sexual harassment are millennia of cultural conditioning that undermines her practical interests. "Whether we know it or not, whether we have read them or not, whether we believe them or don't, our daily lives take direction from stories that are hundreds, even thousands of years old," writes Elizabeth Lesser, the cofounder of the nonprofit educational organization the Omega Institute for Holistic Studies.[2] In her book *Cassandra Speaks*, Lesser examines the origin stories of Western cultures—patriarchal narratives at their most foundational—and their depictions of women to warn that antiquated narratives continue to disempower us. Eve and Pandora teach us that assertiveness and curiosity in women are both wrong and dangerous. The Greek myths of Persephone and Helen instill the importance of both acquiescence and obedience. And I don't even need to be familiar with Pygmalion and Galatea to have absorbed the power of a submissive white woman with a kick-ass body— certainly not when I came of age with the message rebooted on *Beverly Hills, 90210* and *Melrose Place*.

Our cultural mythologies and their contemporary manifestations are a part of us. That's how culture works: it's inescapable, as are the limited scripts it provides us for navigating our lives. We can intend to push back against male entitlement, but in the moment our own internalized patriarchy trips us up. Nothing comes as easily as it should for the strong, self-respecting woman we know ourselves to be. When the comedy writer Liz Meriwether responded to the inappropriate advances of a powerful man in her industry, she did so with uproarious laughter. "It was not a fun laugh. It was one of those crazy, terrifying laughs," she describes in a personal essay for *The Cut*. "I thought I was like the characters I wrote about—I thought I was a plucky young girl who fought back against injustice. A rebel. A feminist. An avenger," laments Meriwether. "It turned out that I was none of those things."[3]

But it also turns out that those characters are exceptions to the rule, and not our most celebrated female archetypes. Even if Meriwether's plucky girl grows up devouring Beverly Cleary books, a fearless, irrepressibly authentic heroine is a rare treat on a steadfast diet of female submissiveness; Ramona Quimby is no match for a heteropatriarchal culture saturated with representations of women who are accepted, loved, and successful while being—or learning to be—all things pleasing to men.

In his book *Selfie*, the British author Will Storr interviews scores of neuroscientists, psychologists, and other academics in a quest to understand the mechanics behind how we derive our sense of self. The answer is that our culture and its narratives do the bulk of the work for us, ensnaring us in a web of instructions for how to be an acceptable person: how to behave, what to look like, and what to want. Storr explains that through a process much like plagiarism, we pull directly from our cultural narratives to create an *ideal* of who we believe ourselves to be. "The brain is a storyteller and it's also a hero-maker—and the hero that it makes is you . . . stealing ideas from the stories that surround it, then incorporating them into its self," he writes.[4] Put differently, we *are* our stories.

This begs an important question: What does it mean for women and girls that the stories upon which their psyches are so fundamentally reliant were born of a culturally heteropatriarchal world—a world that for thousands of years has been scarce on stories in which women drive the plot by their own agency or are extolled for decisively putting male entitlement in check? It means that when a woman wants to do just that—when she wants to stop a man's inappropriateness—things can get precarious. Having spent a lifetime absorbing the wrong scripts, she can find herself scrambling, responding in the moment in ways that weren't at all what she wanted.

Take for example what happened to Charlize Theron in the mid-'90s, when she went to the home of a Hollywood director to discuss potential work. He greeted her at the door in silk pajamas, invited her in to have a drink, and proceeded to rub her leg. She extricated herself from the situation ever so gently by offering polite apologies. "I was in my car driving away, and I just kept hitting the steering wheel," she told Terry Gross years later on NPR's *Fresh Air*. "I was really emotional about it because I couldn't understand where the behavior came from. I was raised with an incredibly strong mother figure."[5]

Theron's mother, Gerda, who worked in road construction, had shown her daughter that women could be power brokers in male-dominated industries. She showed her how to run a farm in apartheid South Africa that is said to have treated the Black people living and working on the land as welcome family. She showed her fifteen-year-old daughter how to defend herself by killing Theron's alcoholic father the night he came home unloading his gun at them. And shortly after that, she urged her daughter to put herself first by leaving home to pursue a once-in-a-lifetime modeling opportunity in Italy. So, yeah, it's reasonable to think Gerda's daughter would grow up to *not* apologize to her sexual harasser. (It's also reasonable to wonder who will play Charlize Theron in the movie about Charlize Theron.)

"Nothing in my past made me feel like, well, then, of course this is why I would apologize and why I would kind of react in this meek way with this guy and not say anything," continued Theron. "And it took me a really long time to realize that that was a cultural influence, that it wasn't necessarily from how I was raised. But it was almost like instilled in me that that's just kind of what you did."

This kind of self-awareness doesn't come easily. Rather than acknowledge that we might have responded in an encounter anti-thetically to who we prefer believing ourselves to be, or accept what little control we actually exerted over our circumstances, we're inclined to tell ourselves a more favorable version of events. We get creative and concoct justifications for our behavior. In fact, we'll embrace humiliation, failure, and self-blame long before we'll question our own autonomy and free will.

The process by which we unconsciously fictionalize the events of our lives, filling in holes to make our stories and identities more coherent, is a mentally healthy one.[6] In the 1960s, the neurosci-entist Michael Gazzaniga led a study at the California Institute of Technology concerning what neuroscientists call our "interpreter," or what most of us might think of as our inner voice. It's in the brain's left hemisphere, which is the side responsible for creating meaning and putting information into context. The right side of our brain has no such mechanism. Gazzaniga looked at severe epi-leptics whose seizures had been treated by a surgery that severed the connection between the brain's two hemispheres, so that no information passed between them. Gazzaniga wanted to know what would happen when information fed only to their left side conflicted with information fed only to their right.

His team did wild variations of the following experiment involv-ing each patient's right and left fields of view as they stared at the center of a monitor. To one man's left hemisphere, and only the left, the image of a chicken claw was shown on the left side of the screen. To his right hemisphere, and only his right, an image of snow was flashed. Researchers then asked him to choose one image from a selection of cards to go with each of the images he'd just been shown. The man chose a chicken to go with the picture he was aware of having seen (the chicken claw) and a snow shovel to go with the one he was unaware of having seen (the snow). When asked why he selected those specific images, he said: "The chicken claw goes with the chicken, and you need a shovel to clean out the chicken shit."[7] With no conscious memory to explain why he'd chosen the shovel, his brain invented a story to fill the space.

Such improbable connections were seen throughout the study. When a woman's right hemisphere was flashed the picture of a pinup girl and her left hemisphere wasn't shown anything, she began to giggle. When asked why, she told the researchers that their equipment was "funny."[8] Importantly, subjects' ability to conjure explanations out of thin air had nothing to do with the separation of their brains' hemispheres; their prior surgeries merely allowed Gazzaniga to isolate the tendency and study it directly. This kind of unconscious fictionalizing, what scientists call "confabulation," has been established in multiple studies since, with research also showing that we do it spontaneously for unexpected behavior that causes us distress.[9]

When women respond to male overtures in surprising ways, and unconsciously grasp for a sense of autonomy, the explanations that make the easiest sense are the ones in which we've spent our lives swimming. Prior to the #MeToo movement, the stories we had heard about sexual misconduct always portrayed it with clear-cut plot progressions: the woman responded immediately, either with a slap, with a forceful *no*, or by fleeing in distress. If she didn't clearly object, then it was a story about a woman who was either using sex to her advantage or who was simply "up for it." These limited storylines had hamstrung our ability to protect nothing less than our sense of self.

I was in my forties the first time I heard a story about rape involving a woman who physically froze in response—what psychologists

call "tonic immobility." Physically freezing is one of our brain's pri-
mary responses to fear, and it's among the most frequent reactions—
maybe *the* most frequent reaction—to sexual assault. Yet the most
familiar narrative we have about rape involves a desperate physical
struggle to the end, which psychologists tell us is statistically rare.[10]
Where does that leave the victim who felt paralyzed, who didn't
fight? How can she be expected to cope with her abuse when
our narratives run so contrary to reality? In the space between
our patriarchal narratives and the lived experiences of women is
a world of harm.

"A Kind of *Lolita* Thing"

Carmen was twenty-six years old and in graduate school studying
journalism when she began interning for Charlie Rose. He pulled
her aside, as he had me, to say that he was looking to hire a new
producer focused on international content—someone he could
travel well with. To test their potential for a working relationship,
he invited Carmen to accompany him to San Francisco for one of
the show's on-location interviews.

Carmen had wanted to work for Charlie since she was a sopho-
more in college after seeing his interview with Charles Manson and
being blown away by the "compassion" she said he brought to his
conversations. In her mind, Charlie Rose could do no wrong. And
that status wasn't necessarily diminished by his keen and uninhib-
ited proclivity for young women. "From day one, you could just
smell it. He was so open and didn't hold back," she told me. Carmen described feeling like her youth and attractiveness were to her
advantage and that she had a power in her possession that was "a
kind of *Lolita* thing." As for the job that Charlie was dangling, she
was confident that she could keep him both happy and in line. "You

don't want it to be sexual, but you know there's an undercurrent in the interactions, and you think you can manage it."

Once in San Francisco, Charlie summoned her to his hotel room. When she arrived and took a seat on the edge of his bed, he went into the bathroom, leaving the door open. Carmen told me that the reality of her predicament struck her with the clank of his belt buckle hitting the bathroom floor as he proceeded to shower about five feet away from her. She didn't know if the open door was an invite to join or to gander, but she knew with certainty that she'd overestimated her ability to control things. "I had been so stupid," she said.

She, of course, had not been stupid. But like many of us, Carmen had been conditioned by a patriarchal narrative so omnipresent that we default to it for easy answers, whatever the context or power differentials at play—namely, that a woman's only proven and permissible superpower is her sex appeal. It's a law so universal it may as well be etched upon cuneiform tablets, and it's how Carmen's sense of autonomy and self-preservation in a questionable situation came to rely on "a kind of *Lolita* thing." I know from personal experience that being alone with one's sexual harasser can feel like being caged with a haggard circus bear, and that sometimes our receptivity and pleasantness are fueled by fear. But this truth does not negate the fact that in the vast and varied expanse of our encounters with sexual misconduct, our responses are shaped by both fear *and* cultural conditioning.

We are so inundated by images and stories depicting a woman's sex appeal as empowering that we would be remiss not to question its impact on our behavior. More specifically, we should question the times we may have presumed our own desirability was a means of asserting control. How willful were our smiles and our change in posture? Or did we recast something involuntary and culturally conditioned as intentional, even strategic, so that we could comfort ourselves with a sense of sway over our circumstances? Despite its prevalence, sexual harassment is rarely something for which we've prepared. When confidence comes so naturally in our own ability to handle tricky situations, why bother thinking through the specifics on how we might respond to unwanted male overtures? But in the moment, it's never that easy, and we frequently fall back on what the patriarchy has long scripted. For women, that's protecting the male ego, maintaining the tenor of the relationship, and being pleasing.[11]

Particularly in the beginning of my experience with Charlie, I provided him with exactly the cheerfulness and receptivity he wanted while framing it as my own choice—my own power. It wasn't what I *wanted* to be doing, but it came naturally and felt wiser and safer than shutting things down. So long as I was pleasing, so long as I kept smiling, I felt like I was managing the situation. My entire adult dating life I never had enough confidence to ever once ask a man out, and yet I presumed myself to be craftily using the je ne sais quoi of my sex appeal to keep the most powerful man I had ever known in check. This was delusional. But far more so, it was understandable.

In 1972, the MIT humanities professor Cynthia Griffin Wolff published a paper in which she examined the female stereotypes found in English literature since the Renaissance. Wolff argued that these stereotypes illustrated the extent to which women in fiction, even when elevated to a central character, are created either to serve men's needs or to relay a cautionary message about what happens to the women who don't. One of the stereotypes, known as the "sensuous woman," is bad news for men insofar as she wields legitimate power over them with her sex appeal—a power that she's ultimately vilified for using. Critically, however, she's the only one of Wolff's female archetypes capable of derailing a man's agenda.

With a power of her own, the sensuous woman lives on today in modern stories, as do the other, less threatening stereotypes: the "virtuous woman," who is good and pure; the "sentimental woman," who is an emotional train wreck; and the "liberated woman," who is intelligent and ambitious but struggles both romantically and logistically to juggle everything she wants in life (think Sandra Bullock in a romantic comedy). No matter which stereotype, the danger is in how we, as women, have internalized it. Our lives come to imitate the art. "A stereotype may become, by a sort of perversity, an image of reality that even women seek to perpetuate," Wolff writes.[12]

"It didn't occur to me to do anything other than respond with vague encouragement, or what an objective observer from the outside would say was flirting. But there was like a disincentive to respond neutrally," a thirty-eight-year-old woman told me about the inappropriate emails she began exchanging with her boss. He was married, generally pleasant, and rarely in the office. She had neither an interest in him, nor in remaining long with the company. "I felt like I was winning at something, like I was gaining some kind of an advantage, and all because he was taking that kind of a liking to me."

To be clear: it is a wonderful, necessary thing to feel desired, and an equally wonderful, necessary thing to express one's sensuality— when experienced with mindful intention. But when these things instead turn on with the kind of autopilot that women can feel in an encounter, it's because we've been conditioned to a level of female performativity that, if not unnoticed, is too often dismissed as a necessary tool of female agency in an imperfect, sexist world. We know this latter narrative all too well.

A Chicago woman told me about working as a business

consultant in her twenties and how frequently she sensed male clients being let down the moment they realized they were meeting with her and not her male boss. "I remember having this sense of *Okay, in addition to being smart, articulate, and informed, I'm going to have to use my feminine wiles to get what I want here. And maybe if I cross my legs just so, right at this angle, perhaps that puts me in a greater position of power.*" She described feeling in control of the situation and always having a "hard no" at her disposal.

Such confidence is common in women's stories, and the more I heard us describing ourselves as totally in control of circumstances involving men who could potentially harm us, the more I came to question it. Sure, women can and do put definitive ends to men's misbehavior. But it's also true that nobody ever says, *I didn't think I could handle it if he became inappropriate.* Nobody. This fact and the detriments it can beget are powerfully illustrated by the story of Melissa Thompson, who met with Harvey Weinstein at his New York offices in 2011.[13]

Thompson surreptitiously took video of the meeting. The scene is shot at desk level, from her laptop, and begins with Thompson, a brunette with dark-rimmed glasses, looking into the camera. She is twenty-eight years old and expecting to meet with the producer and his marketing team to pitch her tech start-up's media platform. Weinstein, however, shows up alone. She stands up to greet him as he is heard telling his employees not to interrupt. Thompson's torso in a fitted dress stands alone in the camera frame when Weinstein's oversize undershirt barges in. She extends her hand and he swipes it aside to hug her, a pleasantry that requires her to awkwardly stretch her torso up and over his considerable stomach. He rubs his palms up and down her back. They sit. He asks if he's allowed to flirt.

"Um . . . we'll see," says Thompson. "A little bit."

"A little bit, not much, right? Okay, then I won't." His tone has shifted to that of a spiteful, ego-bruised sixteen-year-old. "So, what do you want, anyway?"

She starts her presentation with a bit of flattery. He's such a busy man, in charge of so many big things, that she thinks her product could be useful. And as soon as she begins demonstrating on her laptop how the platform works, he appears to start rubbing her legs outside the frame. "You just tell me what I can do and when it's going to happen," he says. "It's fun when we do this."

Thompson does not respond in kind, but she is responding warmly—and with a slight air of seductiveness. She shows him how the platform could reach the target audience on Facebook for his new movie about Marilyn Monroe. She tries humor, leaning in and pushing his shoulder to quip, "Data is so hot, right?" This brief, flirtatious gesture only makes him more aggressive.

"It *is* hot. You're hot. Let me have a little part of you. Give it to me," he insists while grabbing at her under the table.

During a segment on Sky News, a reporter seated with Thompson paused the video to ask her if she thought she might have encouraged Weinstein. "I don't think I purposely encouraged him," she says. She explains that she tried to volley with him by returning whatever he said, but in a way that felt safer. "There was a combination of confidence and naivete that led me to this dynamic that we see now," she tells the reporter. "I worked on Wall Street before I went to business school, and I worked in an environment that was heavily male dominated. I thought I could handle it."

Rather than accept a reality in which she was a disposable object, Thompson seemingly told herself a story involving a young, resourceful woman cunning enough to outfox a licentious older man. The story downplayed the danger she confronted while masking her own objectification as empowerment. Hours after her sales presentation, Thompson met Weinstein at the Tribeca Grand Hotel, where she believed that he would be signing a contract. Instead, she says he raped her.

"Babe in Waiting"

A longtime friend messaged me in 2019 in the wake of Luke Perry's death, which had inspired her to begin rewatching *Beverly Hills, 90210*. The television drama, the first of its kind to be marketed toward adolescents, was hugely popular during our high school years. The issues it addressed were often serious—alcoholism, depression, suicide, pregnancy—but its cast of all-white female characters lacked both depth and assertiveness. They also all looked remarkable in bikinis, save for the supersmart, progressively minded editor of the school paper, who never wore them, nor seemed to ever have a boyfriend, or even so much as a convincing love interest.

"I'm suddenly rethinking a lot about our formative years," wrote my friend. "They were so fucked up! I was such a victim of needing to be the cool girl that I was a fucking misogynist."

If millennia of patriarchal narratives undermining women's own autonomy weren't bad enough, there came the '90s: a decade when reductive, hypersexualized, consumeristic narratives of womanhood took hold of our culture, successfully conflating women's sexual objectification with their own empowerment. If we are our stories—and we know that we are—the '90s made us *all* fucking misogynists.

The '90s bridged the culture gap between 1980s Janet Jackson singing about her control in a bulky pantsuit and 2000s Janet Jackson having a white boy fifteen years her junior tear the black leather off her bedazzled areola. It was when Victoria's Secret went boom, lingerie went mainstream, and the thong became vogue. It was when we learned words like "MILF" and "tramp stamp"; when men got Viagra and women discovered the rabbit. It was when porn wormed its way into every household via the internet, henceforth shaping teenage boys' understanding of sex as well as their expectation that adult vaginas be hairless. The '90s were marked by sex positivity, sex scandals, sex tapes, and generally just a lot more sex.[14]

According to Filipa Melo Lopes, a lecturer in feminist philosophy at the University of Edinburgh, the cultural shift in mainstream thought about feminist issues from the '80s to the '90s was, in a word, profound. In the '80s, feminist "sex wars" had raged between the likes of BDSM-practicing leatherdykes and the feminist lawyer Catharine A. MacKinnon, who, along with radical feminist Andrea Dworkin, had sought to restrict pornography on the grounds that it violated women's civil rights. If anything united these feminist factions, it was fundamental rejection of mainstream ideals about sex and femininity. "But by the mid-'90s, *nobody* talks about whether you should ban porn or not," Melo Lopes told me. "There's this sense that we've won the war and can stop talking about feminist issues. Women can now do anything if they put their minds to it: you can even choose the right shoes and become Carrie Bradshaw."[15]

Indeed, the mantra "Women can do anything" had emerged prior to the debut of *Sex and the City* in 1998—and only served to obfuscate a status quo that was becoming increasingly more sexist. In our neoliberal, so-called postfeminist world of equal opportunity came unlimited possibilities. Adolescent girls were fed this message in the form of "girl power," a slogan attributed to the Spice Girls, who told us what we wanted—what we *really, really* wanted—which, shocker, was nothing that might legitimately challenge the existing social hierarchy.* There was no need to change a system that took us into account, as indicated by the previous decades' enormous gains for women in terms of workplace equality and reproductive rights, and the record number of women now holding political office. Thanks to the hard-fought battles of the boomer women before us and the insistence by many of our second-wave feminist mothers that we were equal to our male peers, we actually *did* believe that we could do anything. This faith, however, was undermined by the fact that we also wanted to be liked, even loved.

In her book *Want Me: A Sex Writer's Journey into the Heart of Desire*, sex journalist Tracy Clark-Flory writes unflinchingly about growing up in the hypersexualized '90s and early aughts and how she was compelled to conflate her self-worth with her own desirability. She shares the story of being fifteen and discovering her father's pornography in the browsing history of his computer. The women she saw striking poses of ecstasy had augmented breasts, plump lips, fake eyelashes, and long, billowing blond hair. "These women represented everything that my dad had long told me didn't matter," she writes. "*High heels are crippling. Makeup is unnecessary. Plastic surgery is unfortunate. Shaving your legs is silly. A woman's most attractive feature is her brain.*" As she stared at the images that contradicted all she had been taught, Clark-Flory internalized that there was something inherently problematic about her: "I was a

---

* The term "girl power" came from the feminist punk band Bikini Kill, who published a zine titled such. The band was a part of riot grrrl, the feminist punk movement of the '90s that used music, zines, and an anti-capitalist "do it yourself" ethos to demand sexual equality in a world that wanted us to believe it had already been accomplished. Riot grrrl and its biggest bands (e.g., Bikini Kill, Bratmobile, and Heavens to Betsy) never went mainstream, but their spirit and messaging were appropriated into the less radical, more commercial, patriarchy-friendly form of "girl power" that we all know today.

girl who liked men, and men—even the good ones—liked *this*." She cried at the realization. Then printed out some of the photos, took them to her room, and masturbated while imagining herself as one of the models.[16]

In 1994, my junior year of high school, Mary Pipher sounded an alarm in her book *Reviving Ophelia,* in which she argued that adolescent girls were now needing medical help not because of individual pathologies but because of a "girl-poisoning culture."[17] Pipher linked the depiction of women in advertising, teen magazines, television shows, and movies to an increasing inability among teenage girls to live authentically. Adolescence had always been difficult, but this was a new kind of psychological harm, and it was leading to an alarming rise in eating disorders, depression, self-mutilation, and suicide attempts. Like Shakespeare's ingenue Ophelia, driven to her death by a wish to please both her father and her lover, teenagers and young women were racked by contradicting pressures. As Pipher put it: "Be beautiful, but beauty is only skin deep. Be sexy, but not sexual. Be honest, but don't hurt anyone's feelings. Be independent, but be nice. Be smart, but not so smart that you threaten boys."[18] In other words, be anything but true to yourself.

Girls coming of age today don't have it easy, either. Psychologists, including Pipher, note that an upward trend in female adolescent mental health—one stemming from responses developed in the '90s—made an alarming U-turn in 2007 with the advent of the iPhone.[19] But as all adolescents continue living media-saturated lives, the '90s stand out for their effectiveness at providing highly potent, highly reductive representations of women. "Mainstream" media was still powerful in a way that it no longer is. Entertainment was a more unified pop culture experience than today's world of streaming options and social media.[20] We still rented movies from actual stores and watched shows when they aired on a major network. We watched more television than today's youth, and we had fewer things to watch, which depicted fewer kinds of people in fewer sets of situations.[21] Not until the 2010s did television and movie narratives begin to diversify in any meaningful way, say cultural critics.[22] And although there's still *very* far to go, by comparison to today, media in the '90s was about as white, straight, and cisgendered as a night at Mar-a-Lago.

This was the decade when housemates looked like Jennifer Aniston or Courteney Cox, female bosses looked like Heather Locklear, lawyers looked like Calista Flockhart, orthopedic surgeons looked like Cameron Diaz, off-shift prostitutes looked like Julia Roberts, vampire slayers looked like Sarah Michelle Gellar, and the woman who would save us from a deadly riptide looked like Pamela Anderson. High school girls were played by Tiffani Amber Thiessen, Jennie Garth, or Alicia Silverstone, and if their appearance was that of Brittany Murphy or Drew Barrymore, the storyline incorporated a dramatic physical makeover upon which their social acceptance hinged. The message was on the screen: Be anything you want, so long as you're hot. Even Elizabeth Berkley, who played the overachieving, straight-A student Jessie Spano on *Saved by the Bell*, qualified, immediately upon graduation, to appear topless in the movie *Showgirls*.

Meanwhile, the "normal" women on our television sets were being pilloried and shamed, beginning the decade with Anita Hill and ending with Monica Lewinsky. Real-life lawyers could look like Marcia Clark, the highly accomplished prosecutor in the O. J. Simpson case, but their legs, hair, and outfits would be ranked and ridiculed daily. One can assume Janet Reno was too focused on serving as our first female attorney general to care about her portrayal on *Saturday Night Live* as an unattractively tall, socially awkward, lesbian control freak played by Will Ferrell in a recurring skit about her basement dance parties.

There was not-so-fine print attached to the mantra "Women can do anything!" We absolutely could—so long as we had exceptionally thick skin. In her book *90s Bitch: Media, Culture, and the Failed Promise of Gender Equality*, journalist Allison Yarrow examines how the decade systematically reduced any woman with power to her fuckability. Yarrow writes that the derogation was "so pervasive, so woven through every aspect of the 90s narrative, that it can actually be tough to spot."[23] From Hollywood to Washington, and with the help of a nascent cable news industry, "Women's careers, bodies, and families were skewered. Nothing was off limits."[24]

I can recall watching a 1992 "Wayne's World" cold open on *Saturday Night Live* in which Wayne and Garth went through their Top 10 list for the upcoming Clinton presidency. Number three was "THE GORE DAUGHTERS," then fifteen-year-old Kristin and nineteen-year-old Karenna Gore, to whom the stoner duo lifted their pelvises off the sofa with an in-unison "Schwing!" And number two on the list? None other than thirteen-year-old Chelsea Clinton. Wayne described her adolescence as "unkind," while Garth was quick to assure us that she could turn out to be a "babe in waiting."[25] It would not be the only time on a national medium that the adolescent daughter of the leader of the free world was reduced to her fuckability. Worse still, I had watched with a sense of awe that girls my own age could command such attention.

Studies unequivocally show that when adolescent girls and women are exposed to the objectification of other women, they are more likely to objectify themselves.[26] We need to question how the '90s impacted women's self-perception and their ability to craft their own protagonism. Where did the decade leave us when we reached for a sense of control but found ourselves sexualized and diminished? Did we, as we so frequently do in dubious circumstances, change the story to something more flattering?

If the 2000s were any indication, it seems like many of us did. The phenomenon of women joining in their own sexual objectification, even celebrating it as female empowerment, is what writer Ariel Levy refers to as "raunch culture" in her 2005 book *Female Chauvinist Pigs*. In it, Levy examines how, within a matter of some thirty years, women went from picketing *Playboy* to wearing the bunny logo as a badge of their own liberation. Among the causes, she cites long-unresolved differences between the women's movement and the sexual revolution, a state of affairs indicating how far women still have to go. Meanwhile, editors at popular magazines had shared a different take than Levy, citing the cultural shift as proof that the feminist project had been achieved. "We'd *earned* the right to look at *Playboy*; we were *empowered* enough to get Brazilian bikini waxes," she writes. "Women had come so far, I learned, we no longer needed to worry about objectification or misogyny. Instead, it was time for us to join the frat party of pop culture, where men had been enjoying themselves all along."[27]

In the raunchy world of the 2000s, the reductive narratives of '90s womanhood had assumed a new, performative element: a pervasive compulsion among women to demonstrate their "hotness," be they college students, Olympic athletes, or female executives. In 2003, Katie Couric—the first solo female anchor of a nightly news program, one of the highest-paid individuals in broadcast history, and a woman who has interviewed presidents and prime ministers alike—sought hot-babe approval while guest-hosting *The Tonight Show* for Jay Leno. Donning a low-cut black dress, she points to her breasts and exclaims, to the audience's delight, "These are actually real!" She tells them she wanted to wear something more fun than her usual attire: "you know, a little sexier." She twirls around in solicitation of applause. When she takes her seat, men with power tools trot out in a staged bit, removing the front panel from Leno's desk to give an unimpeded view of Couric's sculpted legs. Levy references the late-night appearance as an enactment of what it takes to be hot: the projection of eagerness and the promise that any attention your physicality receives is welcome. She writes, "It is not enough to be successful, rich, and accomplished: Even women like Couric . . . women at the pinnacle of their fields, feel compelled to display their solicitude."[28]

If the 2000s were the frat party, the '90s were a pre-party of Zima and Jell-O shots that helped get us there—a point along the evening's trajectory by which we can now, with hindsight, see how circumstances changed for women and girls, making them more susceptible to their own self-objectification.

CHAPTER FOUR

Consent Contextualized

Marie-Louise Friedland was alone with a man in his kitchen when he began kissing her in a way that she found repulsive. Not helping matters was the fact that he held immense power over her career. "I thought, *Okay, I'm in no way physically attracted to him, but maybe I should be more patient and kind*," she told me. "I should have been a crazy bitch and just flipped the table over. But I couldn't. I just couldn't. So I rationalized it to get through it: I told myself he was trying to date me to make it not so bad . . . I already felt so cornered."[1]

I had reached out to Friedland after learning of her experience in the *New York Times*. She was twenty-five years old at the time, working in Austin's fine-dining industry and training toward her goal of becoming a certified sommelier. He was a forty-something master sommelier—the highest rank of wine expertise—and the top wine buyer for Whole Foods. Friedland was preparing to take a rigorous, three-part sommelier exam for which it was possible he would be her proctor. There's no standard study guide for becoming a part of the sommelier world. The process relies heavily, if not entirely, on mentorship from established sommeliers, especially when it comes to the blind-tasting portion of the exam. So when the bad kisser first offered to help Friedland study in private tasting sessions at his home, she felt incredibly fortunate—as well as torn. She found him arrogant. He'd also already kissed her once before, late one evening after having a drink with others in the industry, when, against her protest, he insisted on walking her to her car. Her intentions since had been to make it clear that she didn't want anything physical with him. But now she had a decision to make: Be presumptuous enough to say no, or naive enough to say yes? Forgo a professional opportunity, or decide that you can handle it if he tries again? Be unreceptive to the friendliness of someone with influence, or have the confidence that you can maintain a relationship on professional terms?

Friedland accepted his offer with a faith in her ability to control the situation. But once he went to kiss her, she was consumed by fear—a fear of his influence, of hurting his ego, of upsetting him and ostracizing herself from Austin's small and familial wine community. She couldn't muster a response beyond passivity. She would soon return to his house for more tasting sessions, most of which devolved quickly into sex she didn't want. She reframed these encounters as a fledgling courtship, despite that they never went on dates and all their interactions were in secret at his house. Nothing about it felt like a careful, well-intentioned effort at a romance that could account for professional circumstances. Maybe it would all get better, she told herself, if only *she* would give it a chance. "I didn't like the way he kissed. I didn't like the way he touched me," she said. "On some level, I had to be aware that I was forcing it."

Friedland took the sommelier exam in Atlanta, where she could visit her mother and avoid having him as her proctor. She received a top score. But she knew that the Court of Master Sommeliers, which oversaw the process, was a tight-knit boys' club, and she feared that he had intervened to influence the results. She also became paranoid that people in the industry would find out about everything and think that she was using sex to take advantage of him. She did her best to put it out of her mind and to focus on her studies for the next level of accreditation. But things would soon come to a head at a court-related event in Dallas when he invited her for a drink at his hotel bar.

She didn't want to go, but she did—and after only a couple of drinks ended up abnormally drunk. She woke up in his hotel bed, unable to recall how she got there. She could remember only snapshots of their sexual encounter and how physically painful it had been. She grabbed her belongings and left, driving the three and a half hours back to Austin still intoxicated. Everything about the evening had been unwanted, among a larger string of unwanted encounters that had entangled her to a point she could no longer bear. Friedland knew she would never have physical contact with him again, but it took her years as well as therapy to realize that she had lied to herself about the nature of their relationship in order to make the situation feel less threatening.

I asked her if she considered her encounters consensual. "I've been thinking about that a lot," she said. "I didn't say yes and I didn't say no. It all just happened."

That's unfortunately how consent can sometimes feel: like something that *just happened*—something that's devoid of desire, or even intention. It's a green light given by default and not want, an encounter in which we were aware of what we were acquiescing to; we just wish we could have avoided doing so. We consented because of circumstances, which were messy, uncertain, and not what we wanted. We went, in the moment and sometimes long in the aftermath, with whatever felt like our most viable path to self-preservation—the least shitty of shit options.

Yet we cling to a conception of consent that's categorical, something that's either there or it's not. We grant it a simplicity that makes kosher the ethically precarious and keeps uncomfortable questions at bay. Like Friedland, we tell ourselves a story that's easier to live with: what was wholly unwanted or physically coerced gets rendered a miscommunication, a mistake. But if we contextualize these moments and more closely look at how our so-called consent was elicited by the murky and threatening externalities of a patriarchal world, we can better understand how we're harmed by the concept's limitations. More specifically, how rather than protecting and advancing women's own autonomy, it can work to preserve male entitlement.

Some will feel that contextualizing our consent makes a mockery of women's agency and free choice. They might point out, as I have, that women are not defenseless and that responsibility for our choices *and* our mistakes makes each of us a moral agent with the power to say yes or no, and to have sex however and with whomever we choose.[2] To claim otherwise—that we don't mean what we say or do or, worse yet, that we don't *understand* what we say or do—dooms us to haplessness and fragility. I, however, believe that we can affirm women's agency while also considering the context in which it's exercised. Women have power and women wield power. We are not slugs on a salt farm. But while our agency is real, so, too, is the patriarchy in which we exercise it, a world that maintains our precarity—physically, socially, and economically—by design.

Most women know what true and enthusiastic consent is because they've given it. But they've also given something else, something less willful and far more circumstantial. And regardless of how they might feel about it now—victimized, traumatized, slightly weirded out, or completely fine—interrogating this fact with honesty helps us to become better practitioners of consent while also ending an important aspect of our complicity.

"A Bit Tough to Concentrate"

We often use consent as a one-size-fits-all narrative no matter the power differentials at play. Few people would know this better than Addie Zinone, who was a twenty-four-year-old production assistant for NBC's *Today* show when she encountered Matt Lauer.[3] With ambitions to become a broadcast journalist, Zinone got her foot in the show's door in 1998, when she was a college student and secured herself an internship by faxing a letter directly to Katie Couric. From there, she worked her way to becoming a full-time employee, establishing what she has described as positive, professionally supportive relationships with the show's anchors—with the exception of Lauer, who always kept a distance.

So Zinone was caught off guard the first time Lauer, who was forty-two at the time, reached out to her via the office's instant-messaging system. Hey, I hope you won't drag me to personnel for saying this. But you look fantastic, he wrote. She thanked him and then parlayed the exchange into an opportunity to discuss her career. She informed Lauer that she would be leaving the show later that summer to pursue an opportunity in local broadcast news reporting—the kind of experience necessary if she ever wanted to secure a national news spot.[4]

A month passed before Lauer messaged again.

OK . . . NOW YOU'RE KILLING ME . . . YOU LOOK GREAT TODAY!
He added, A BIT TOUGH TO CONCENTRATE. After an hour went by
and Zinone hadn't responded, he messaged, well silence is golden.[5]
She sought to confirm that it was actually him and not someone
playing a joke, finding it hard to believe that he would be so casually
inappropriate. And even after she found out that these comments
were indeed his, she didn't want to embarrass herself by thinking
anything meant more than it did.[6]

Lauer arranged for them to have lunch the next day, which
Zinone framed in her mind as an opportunity to get some career
advice. She had, after all, discussed her professional aspirations
over meals with many others at the show. But she reports that
Lauer's own objectives were evident as soon as she sat down in the
restaurant, and that his come-ons were a lot to process. In an interview with Dianna Pierce Burgess of Press Forward, an organization
dedicated to changing the culture of newsrooms, Zinone described
being overwhelmed, paralyzed with anxiety about how to respond
to the figurehead of an organization to which she had devoted
two years of her life. She acknowledged an undeniable element of
flattery that comes with an industry titan wanting you, while also
explaining that it was more than dampened by the awareness he
had zero concern for her professional well-being.

Back in the office that afternoon, Zinone messaged Lauer to
confide that the lunch had left her struggling. He told her to come
to his dressing room, and to hurry, as he had a car coming to pick
him up in twenty minutes. His intentions were clear, and she went.
They had what she describes as a consensual encounter. Over the
next few months, she would continue to oblige Lauer when he
requested her presence. It was all she could think to do.

"Even as a forty-three-year-old, I think back to my twenty-four-year-old self; I go through every single step of that process, from the first time he texted me and to what actually happened. And would I have done anything differently? And I wouldn't have. Because I wouldn't have *known* to do it differently," she told Burgess. "I went as a willing participant, and I want to always own my part in that . . . I consented. But the larger issue is, what is consent under that power dynamic?"[7]

The answer? A cruelly inadequate concept for describing what happened between her and Lauer.

We're so boxed in by our simplistic, all-or-nothing conception of consent that what Lauer *extracted* from Zinone gets equated with what a woman *gives* when she decides—and enthusiastically expresses—that she wants to have sex with a partner. Consent is also the only narrative Zinone has to differentiate what happened to her from other women's experiences with unwanted physical force or sexual violence. It's likely that Zinone, who went on to complete two tours of duty as an Army staff sergeant in Iraq, feels morally compelled to say that she consented out of a belief in personal responsibility and integrity. But by using the word "consent," she inadvertently shifts the focus of the story to character—*her* character—when the circumstances were paramount to everything that transpired. She didn't acquiesce because she wanted to, or because of some moral failing. She acquiesced because an immensely powerful man pressured her in a professional and cultural context saturated by his entitlement.

Recall that behind every woman's encounter with sexual misconduct there are millennia of cultural conditioning that work to undermine her practical interests. The patriarchy has never provided easily accessible, effective scripts for confronting male entitlement.

That's not how hegemony works. And yet women like Zinone are expected to formulate an instantaneous response, to weigh the pros and cons of all their crappy options and the implications for their careers and livelihoods—and then act decisively. If we even begin to put ourselves in these women's shoes and to imagine the pressure and the dynamics they're confronting, what *exactly* would we expect their response to look like? Simple answers, such as a polite "No, thank you," trivialize the likelihood of professional repercussions as well as a lifetime of internalized patriarchy. They also presume a lucidness and detachment of mind that people rarely, if ever, have during unexpected and threatening circumstances.

When it comes to sexual misconduct in real time, it's just as Lauer described: *a bit tough to concentrate.* To garner the clarity and confidence required to push back against what someone more powerful is putting in motion demands time. The couple of hours Zinone had in the middle of a busy workday to process what was happening—to fully comprehend that one of the most prominent figures at her network, possibly the most prominent figure in the entire broadcast industry, was pressuring her to have sex with him—was simply not enough. Without a pause button for women in any such similar circumstance, going along will often feel more natural, more familiar, and even safer than doing otherwise.

"Obedience is often a reflex, not a rational decision," explains the author and executive coach Ira Chaleff about our instinct to obey authority in circumstances that are overwhelming or involve disparate power dynamics. In his book *Intelligent Disobedience: Doing Right When What You're Told to Do Is Wrong,* Chaleff provides case studies of individuals who went against what was asked of them by authority figures. The two themes salient in these success stories are notably absent from any story I've ever heard about sexual misconduct in real time. The first one is pausing. People took a moment for a deep breath or a big step back in order to calmly think things through. The second one is practice. People had actually practiced what it would take to disobey: they had prepared for doing what they anticipated would in the moment feel counterintuitive. Chaleff likens it to firefighters who practice running into burning buildings under controlled conditions before needing to do the real thing.

How many of us rehearse saying no to powerful men—or, for that matter, any men? Whatever preparation we *have* had certainly pales in comparison to the amount that we've practiced follow- ing patriarchal scripts on how to be a pleasing—and appeasing— woman. It's not hyperbole to say that some of us have spent a lifetime honing what are possibly the most problematic of reflexes required, in the moment, to shut a misbehaving man down. So, yeah, it's reasonable to assume that we might be more sluggish than we'd like at hitting the brakes or that we might find ourselves rolling with things we never wanted.

Dianna May was in her early twenties and starting out at ABC News when she stopped by the office of the network's political director and rising star, Mark Halperin.[8] She needed some informa- tion from him, and he asked that she close the door. "Come over here," he said. Then, gesturing to his lap, he told her, "Sit down and I'll give it to you." When I contacted May after reading about her story in the *Washington Post*, she explained to me that she obliged Halperin, reluctantly, because of his stature at the company. It was brief. He had an erection. When he made the same request three or four more times, she obliged again, feeling an overwhelming sense of shame and confusion each time.

I asked May about the window of deliberation in her first

encounter with him—the few seconds she had to respond to his shocking overture—and how she might think about the intricacies of that moment now. In response, she told me that a few people close to her couldn't understand why she hadn't just said no. They weren't passing judgment, she explained; they just couldn't get their minds around it. Beyond her youth, she didn't have an answer, either. She was just as dumbfounded as her friends were. "Where was my spine?" she said. "Where was the woman my mom had raised?"

Indulging a superior's request to sit on his lap may indeed sound crazy to some. But I've come to believe that had Mark Halperin insisted, as May said he did, I probably would have done the same. And in that moment it would have had less to do with my career than a need to be a cool female peer; to take my work but not myself too seriously; to be warm and not cold; to not read too much into things (lest I be crazy!); to avoid causing a scene; and to be *anything* other than difficult. I also would have proceeded with the belief that I was still the one in charge, that I could just touch my butt down and immediately pop back up, all the while laughing him off and poking fun at his creepiness—because that's how unflappable I was. The reasons to oblige and to just go along are limitless. Whereas a narrative for a woman to do differently, certainly in the moment, is all too elusive.

Consent and Coping

The repeat encounters that both Addie Zinone and Dianna May had with their abusers is a common pattern. In the aftermath of such an unwanted experience, women move on in whatever way can protect their sense of self and well-being. A single so-called consensual moment can become a corrosive plot point in a woman's story that she struggles to incorporate, as the toll becomes ongoing.

When I look back on my own most unwanted or borderline coercive sexual encounters, the more questionable my consent, the more I could sometimes be involuntarily drawn back to the men. This was especially true if they were a part of my broader social circle, such as a classmate or the brother-in-law of a good friend. I'd meet up with them again, not sure why I was there. I didn't want to see them, but I wanted a different note on which to leave things—and my story could still change if the situation was ongoing. My attempts were never successful. I also realize now that I occasionally went beyond trying to reframe what had transpired by instead trying to completely deny it.

After I went on the record against Charlie, a lawyer I had dated messaged me his support:

Glad u spoke out so this BS can end, he wrote, and then suggested I sue. This was an audacious response, and it incensed me for reasons I had yet to grapple with. *You came closer to raping me than anyone*, I thought—before thinking about it some more. He had once held my arms behind my back as I kicked and yelled for him to stop, which he did, and that was the crux of my story. But receiving his message had triggered the memory, along with a willingness to process it more completely: the fact that he didn't let go of me until after he had penetrated me and come, by which point I had long stopped kicking and yelling and lain motionless.

Memory, according to neuroscientists, is about what serves us moving forward—what information is most vital to our future welfare and preservation—and that doesn't include a mindful awareness of one's own sexual assault. Dr. Jim Hopper, who specializes in psychological trauma at Harvard Medical School, writes that "while people may have the superficial abstract stories they tell themselves and others about their worst traumas, that's not because the worst details have been lost. It's often because they *don't want* to remember them, and don't (yet) feel safe to remember them."9 The broader context of my rape was that it happened hours after I'd flown across an ocean to see this man in Asia, where he was on a work trip. It was the first day of a weeklong vacation together in a chaotic city that I didn't feel like navigating alone. When I stormed out of the bedroom, he downplayed things, and it wasn't long until I began questioning my own version of events. I stayed that night, then the rest of the week, and let him visit me a month later in New York. My rape, by definition, was not consensual. But that's not how I had retroactively filed it away, when I made things more manageable for myself by labeling it a blundered, overly aggressive sexual encounter and nothing more.

My realization was stranger than it was upsetting. What concerned me wasn't my victimhood as much as my grasp of reality. What else had I avoided processing? How else was I among statistics I thought only applied to other women? Those of us who mislabel our assaults as something more benign are identified by researchers through surveys that describe the circumstances of rape but avoid using the actual word. In one 1996 study, psychologists looked at the behavioral patterns of women who had acknowledged being raped versus those who had not. The emotional well-being of those who didn't recognize their rape as such fared significantly better than those who did, who exhibited symptoms of post-traumatic stress disorder. And despite the honest recognition of what had transpired, one-third of these women still maintained relationships with their rapists, while a quarter of them had continued to sleep with them.10

More telling still, according to a meta-analysis of twenty-eight studies of women and girls fourteen years and older, the majority of rape victims don't believe they've been raped. Sixty percent of those who had nonconsensual sex, either by force, threat, or incapacitation, didn't acknowledge having been raped at all.[11] A similar kind of wishful thinking is also found among rapists who don't believe that they actually raped anyone. Anonymous surveys of American men consistently show that so long as the words "rape" or "sexual assault" are not used to describe the encounter, male subjects will freely acknowledge having had nonconsensual sex or having penetrated a woman against her will while remaining steadfast in their belief that what transpired bore no resemblance to a rape.[12] As for my own rapist, I have no doubt that he thought his actions that night were justified, and that years later he didn't think twice before commending me for speaking out against lesser injustices.

If the ghost of radical feminist Andrea Dworkin could snap her fingers and enable everyone who had ever raped or been raped to wholly appreciate the truth of it, she'd be exposing more than the ubiquity of sexual violence and coercion; she'd be exposing the extent to which our self-assurance is built on fictionalizations. We all edit our stories as our mental and emotional well-being demands. For many women, this also means behaving toward their perpetrator in a way that can keep open the possibility of a plot twist, maybe even a happy ending.

"That I fraternized with my attackers for the remainder of high school and even into college does not make my account suspect, it makes it textbook," the author Jessica Knoll wrote about going on a date with one of the three guys who gang-raped her when she was fifteen years old. "When my rapist asked me out, two years later, I was *grateful* . . . I still thought this person could offer me something by way of healing."[13]

The assault happened at a house party in high school while Knoll was intoxicated, struggling in and out of consciousness. The trauma would go on to inform her 2015 novel and 2022 Netflix movie adaptation, *Luckiest Girl Alive*, in which the protagonist is similarly raped by three classmates and, as also experienced by Knoll, left to confront a community of peers who could only comprehend what happened as the willful machinations of a "trash slut" (the words scrawled on the inside of her locker). Knoll knew that her experience had not been consensual. She even accused one of her assailants of having raped her before apologizing in fear of the potential social repercussions. She suffered due to a lack of understanding about what rape could look like and who could commit it—ignorance to which our all-or-nothing conception of consent is foundational.

Two years after her assault, Knoll would go on a date with one of her rapists. Three years after that, she would make out with him at a party. When she eventually decided to speak publicly about her gang rape, she panicked that these facts would discredit her. But as she would later acknowledge in *The Cut*, "I owe it to my younger self, and to the younger women who stay silent because their behavior does not align with the inaccurate archetype of a sexual assault victim. Women who play nice with their abusers are not cowards. We are not opportunistic, and we are not untrustworthy. We are the clear majority."[14]

As public awareness regarding what constitutes sexual abuse and predatory behavior has shifted in recent years, there's hope that we've also become better equipped, supported, and more inclined to confront the sometimes circumstantial nature of our consent. When a New York jury convicted Harvey Weinstein in 2020 of two felony sex crimes—crimes committed against women who *also* acknowledged having had consensual sex with him and having maintained relations on friendly terms after their assaults—it was a watershed moment indicating that our legal institutions could account for the narrative complexity of both consent and victimhood. We deserve to extend that same awareness, indeed compassion, to ourselves.

Generation X Marks the Spot

The #MeToo movement conjured a generational divide when it came to women's agency and sexual misconduct: a supposed split between older women who believe they'd willingly made compromises and younger women eager to call out abuse. Most frequently depicted as a rift between boomers and millennials, the two sides supposedly disagree over what constitutes mistreatment versus, say, life?

"We were strong in a way that so many modern girls are weak," wrote Caitlin Flanagan in the *Atlantic*, about women like herself who grew up in the '70s. "Apparently there is a whole country full of young women who don't know how to call a cab."[15] The alleged generational disconnect here isn't younger women's preference for ridesharing apps but their inability to sidestep or curtail an unwanted advance. Flanagan was specifically addressing accusations levied by a woman who claimed that the comedian Aziz Ansari had ignored her verbal and nonverbal cues while pressuring her into giving him a blow job. Fifty-year-old CNN reporter Ashleigh Banfield weighed in on the air, telling the anonymous woman: "You had an unpleasant date. And you did not leave. That is on you." Banfield was angry over the harm she believed such "reckless and hollow" accusations would do to the progress #MeToo was making on behalf of all women.[16] Or as former secretary of state Condoleezza Rice told David Axelrod in a televised interview more broadly about the movement: "Let's not turn women into snowflakes."[17]

Meanwhile, boomers have been depicted as out of touch or complacent about their own mistreatment. Among them are second-wave feminists, generally women active in the feminist movement from the 1960s to the late 1980s, whom younger feminists have called out for their unwillingness to dismantle the existing social order that so strongly favors well-off white women. Writing for *Jezebel*, Stassa Edwards described the older vanguard as having "rationalized, normalized, and coded abusive, predatory behavior as flirting, as courtship, as the simple reality of being female or any other marginalized gender."[18]

But the truth is that any such generational divide rarely holds up to scrutiny. According to polling, women of all ages have generally held the same opinions about #MeToo and have reported experiencing sexual harassment to the same degree. The biggest difference is that younger women tend to be more willing than their older counterparts to *report* the sexual harassment—something often chalked up to their increased expectations that workplaces be egalitarian and their confidence that they can find a new job if necessary.[19]

Generally speaking, many differences that get described as "generational" are simply a matter of the stage someone's at in their life. Should, for example, a millennial register her sexual harassment with more alarm than a baby boomer, it's less likely because millennials are inherently more fragile than the case that older women, who have spent many more years of their life in the labor force, have had more time to grow accustomed to—and not be as surprised by—women's mistreatment in the workplace. Generational analysis should always be approached with caution. In his book *The Generation Myth*, Bobby Duffy explains that while the concept of generations can yield important insights into who we are, the topic is too often reduced to lazy thinking that leads to useless if not dangerous assumptions. "Instead," writes Duffy, "we need to carefully unpack the forces that shape us as individuals and societies; the generation we were born into is merely one important part of the story, alongside the extraordinary influence of individual life cycles and the impact of historical events."[20]

What if, rather than looking for a generational divide when it came to our attitudes about female agency, sexism, and abuse, we looked for a point in history when our culture changed, along with our narratives for understanding sexual consent? A point when the messages about our sexual encounters became especially conflicted, personal responsibility absolute, and self-blame inevitable? That point, which struck with the neoliberalism, sex positivity, and female objectification of the '90s, came down mercilessly upon Gen Xers coming of age. We certainly weren't the first or last generation to confront sexual misconduct or gender-based violence, but we were uniquely primed to downplay it.

It's notable that discussions of the supposed generational divide tend to focus on boomers and millennials, leaving out Generation X—those born between 1965 and 1980.* We're a less referenced generation, sometimes even left out of television news graphics that skip straight from boomers to millennials.[21] We're also a relatively smaller cohort. Data as of 2019 put us at 65.2 million, bookended by 71.6 million boomers and 72.1 million millennials.[22] We're what

---

* This age range is defined by the Pew Research Center.

the Pew Research Center calls "America's neglected 'middle child,'" which has nothing to do with our former status as "latchkey kids" who returned from school to empty homes.[23] But even in a national dialogue about women's sexual harassment, the fact that the generation of women largely ignored was precisely the one known for the sexist, demeaning psychological trauma of its adolescence feels about as negligent as it also does . . . oddly appropriate for us Xers.

When Mary Pipher's *Reviving Ophelia* was published in 1994, she was among many voicing concern about the implications of teenage girls developing their sexual agency in a culture saturated with their own sexual objectification. Alarms were similarly rung in 1992 by academic feminists Carol Gilligan and Lyn Mikel Brown with the publication of their book *Meeting at the Crossroads*, which gave voice to the social pressures facing young women and the resulting toll on their psychological health. Developmental psychologist Deborah L. Tolman published a decade's worth of academic articles on adolescent girls' sexual development before writing *Dilemmas of Desire*, a 2002 book addressing the tendency of teenage girls to erase their own agency from their sexual encounters: by instead letting things "just happen," they avoided being either a prude who said no or a slut who said yes. The expert consensus was that adolescent girls were facing many of the same harmful gender ideologies of generations past but with new, more insidious dimensions because of a shift in the cultural climate.

It was also in the '90s that the social and developmental psychologist Lynn Phillips began studying the sexual experiences of female college students, who she believed had learned to downplay male aggression and blur the line between consent and coercion. Phillips's 2000 book *Flirting with Danger* is an in-depth, qualitative study of a diverse group of thirty such students and the contradictions they confronted when it came to their own sexual agency. Raised by second-wave feminists, these young women discussed their sexuality openly, stood vocally against sexual violence, and felt certain they were equal to their male peers. Yet they'd also grown up amid the social conservatism of Reagan, Bush, and the Religious Right's culture war, and an anti-feminist media backlash speciously claiming that gender equality had both been achieved and was now responsible for women's current unhappiness.[24] As exhaustively documented by Susan Faludi in her groundbreaking 1991 book *Backlash: The Undeclared War Against Women*, media-driven scaremongering about the dismal state of liberated women was inescapable. We now reportedly suffered from professional burnout, greater rates of mental illness, and an infertility epidemic. According to *Newsweek*, if we were single, educated, and had reached forty, we had a better chance of dying in a terrorist attack than ever getting married.*

Phillips explained that a threatening, contradictory world manifested itself in the female students' heterosexual encounters, which were muddled elements of flattery and humiliation, empowerment and disempowerment. And through it all, the young women were determined to appear confident and sophisticated—to project that they knew the rules and what they were getting into no matter how conflicted they truly were. They spoke about men they neither cared for nor found attractive, yet to whom they felt beholden.[25] They frequently had remorse and confusion about hookups that had gone further than they wanted, and described instances of coercion or violent force that could read like satirical pieces in *The Onion*: "No, I don't think of it as abuse or victimization or anything, because

---

* *Newsweek* retracted this claim in 2006, acknowledging that the statistics in its explosive 1986 cover story were flawed.

even though it may have looked that way with his hand over my mouth and his hurting me and all, I just don't think I could ever call myself a victim," a twenty-two-year-old student said about the night she lost her virginity to her boyfriend—or when he raped her. "I went into the whole thing willingly, and even though I got hurt, I figured, well . . . this just comes with the territory, I guess."[26]

Phillips wrote that "whereas feminist scholars may speak of male domination and women's victimization as rather obvious phenomena, young women, raised to believe in their own independence, invulnerability, and sexual entitlement, may not so readily embrace such concepts, even as they are raped, harassed, and battered by men." Twenty-seven of the thirty women she interviewed recounted at least one situation fitting the legal definition of "harassment," "battering," or "rape," yet only two of them ever used such terms to describe their experiences—and they used the terms inconsistently, not applying them to other encounters that were similarly coercive and violent.[27] Worse yet, the women regularly blamed themselves. They weren't victims, they explained—but not because of any kind of chin-up-and-move-on-with-it attitude attributed to the boomers before them. Rather, it was because their stories didn't allow for nuance or ambiguity. Everything, from emotional abuse to sexual assault, was a zero-sum game in a narrative that lacked male accountability. Women were either up for sex or they weren't. Their encounters were either normal or dangerous. They were in control or they were victims.

Having gone to college myself in the '90s, this all resonated with me. As a good friend from that time told me about her own questionable, unwanted hookups: "It would never have occurred to me *not* to blame myself." Together, we had made fun of ourselves for the moments with guys we never intended or seemed to have enjoyed—what I now know was humor used to gain a sense of agency. To laugh at a sexual encounter is to confirm its insignificance. Years later, I would talk about Charlie's advances with a similar self-deprecating humor to a couple of my close friends. I needed to acknowledge what was going on, and the only way I knew how was to ignore the darker elements of my story, as well as all the times I had cried alone, and to instead frame things in terms of a pervy old broadcaster I comically found myself putting up with.

The feminist psychologist Laina Bay-Cheng studies women's sexual agency and views our inclination to overlook the more questionable aspects of our encounters with men through the lens of neoliberalism. She believes that our sexual narratives have come to reflect our political ones: couched in terms of personal responsibility and individual choice, and infiltrated by a market rationality of winners and losers. Bay-Cheng coined the term "neo-liberal agency" to describe a certain compulsion that women now feel to demonstrate their sexual control. Regardless of the reality of our sexual experiences, what changed with the political back-drop of the '90s was an increased imperative for us to prove the "unfettered free will" of our sex lives. Gone are the days when women were stigmatized, or "slut-shamed," merely for what was considered promiscuous behavior. Today we're subjected to a new kind of shaming that, according to Bay-Cheng, isn't about being sexually active so much as it's about being sexually out of control. Thus, as a form of self-protection, we'll disregard what we have to about our sexual experiences in order to ensure their perception as consensual.[28]

Bay-Cheng's research identified something else about women's neoliberal agency, which is that, like everything else neoliberal, there must be *haves* and *have-nots*. Young women make sure to highlight their own control relative to others' lack of it. That's how sexual agency, like an SAT prep course, becomes an advantage enjoyed by middle-class white girls. "Girls must draw sharp contrasts between themselves and others, largely through slut-shaming and victim-blaming, in order to prop themselves up," she writes. "Racialized and economically disadvantaged girls are made easy targets for such downward comparisons by race and class-based constructions of them as over-sexed and under-disciplined."[29]

Misdirected blame was part and parcel of the '90s. The cultural and political conditions of the time distorted women's consent in a way that made us ever more vulnerable to sexual abuse—the consequences of which we're still dealing with today.

CHAPTER FIVE

Foot Soldiering in Stilettos

On a winter weekend in 2006, I met two friends for breakfast burri-
tos in Albuquerque's North Valley, which is not to be confused with
the city's South Valley. The South Valley is known to be rougher.
It's where I grew up until the age of nine and where the psychotic
drug kingpin Tuco Salamanca moved crystal meth in the first season
of *Breaking Bad*. But before Albuquerque became the backdrop to
one of the most lauded television series of all time, it was where
Jessica Simpson filmed the far-less-acclaimed *Employee of the Month*,
costarring Dane Cook and Dax Shepard. And that morning, as we'd
heard incessantly advertised on local radio stations, was the movie's
casting call.

We made a post-burrito appearance at the audition because
I insisted it would be a hilarious experience, at least if we did it
together. The truth was that my friends Kat and Ruby couldn't be
extras even if they had wanted. They both had to work. I, however,
had just returned home financially broke from a Fulbright in the

Middle East and had multiple months of unemployed time until I would be starting graduate school. This made me the only one of us actually amenable to the chance that our lark might yield something beyond laughs.

But from the parking lot of the hotel holding the auditions, even the laughs became questionable. The scene was uncomfortably depressing. I've heard that in Los Angeles those who attend background auditions have an ambition that's been grounded by their proximity to the industry. They understand that the essence of their role, should they be selected, is indeed for *background* purposes. Casting calls seemed to unfold differently in a nonindustry city like Albuquerque, where a line that wrapped around the hotel was disproportionately young, female, and scantily clad. Girls from places like the South Valley had exposed midriffs, thickly sheened lips, and bouffant hair. It didn't seem like they were there to be in a Jessica Simpson movie so much as they were there to *be* Jessica Simpson—or, rather, a similarly sexualized iteration of her.

The three of us questioned what we were doing as the line moved quickly. We had our pictures taken and filled out our availability on paper forms, which we handed to a woman who then gave us each a once-over before writing across the top of our papers how we might be of service. When Kat was handed hers back, she broke into hysterical laughter, holding it up for us to see: "GREAT ETHNICITY!" it read in caps. This was no doubt true. Kat's Native American and Japanese ancestry is evidenced by her striking bone structure, including cheekbones that could serve as armrests. Ruby received her form next, and written across the top of it was the one-word question: "Pakistani?" Ruby is Black and at the time kept her hair in a pixie cut that showed off the feminine contours of her face and neckline. Her appearance was many things. But that she looked Pakistani? That was new to us.

I received my typecasting last, also in the form of a question: "Hot babe?" An awkward feeling of part flattery and part shame washed over me. Flattery, I'll admit, because some woman in casting apparently thought I *might* fit an attractive mold of some sort. And shame because of a far more complex reason that involved the larger context at hand—something that had inspired a disconcerting amount of self-objectification among economically vulnerable young women and girls. Receiving the feedback "Hot babe?" was uncomfortable because it made my participation feel intentional, as if I had wanted to use my sexuality all along. I became self-conscious about the tight fit of my jeans and that I had bothered to blow-dry my hair that morning. It wasn't too dissimilar from how I felt the first time Charlie was physically inappropriate with me, when I wondered if I had asked for it.

Kat wanted to see my form, and I begrudgingly showed it to her. She again erupted in laughter, this time over the question marks. "I love that she can't decide!" Kat howled.

Of course, one might argue that, based on notions of white femininity and Eurocentric beauty standards, she could decide well enough where to siphon me, as opposed to my friends of color. And so, as a questionably hot babe, I went on to appear for a hot second in *Employee of the Month*. The scene is shot at a Costco. In it, I stand among a group of women in a checkout line as Dax Shepard, our cashier and object of our collective hankering, scans the entirety of a shopping cart in record time. His character has us shrieking in adoration and fanatically cheering him on, because apparently—for the sake of the plot—there's nothing women find sexier than a man with a big barcode gun.

In the years after the movie's release, I'd occasionally hear from someone asking if they had just seen me jumping up and down for

Shepard. I would play it down, describing it as the unintentional result of brunching with my comically spontaneous girlfriends. When a friend from home posted on Facebook that her husband had just paused the television to ask if that could be me, I replied, "Friends don't let friends watch Jessica Simpson movies!" I apparently believed myself above the pop star and the kind of reality TV celebrity she represented. In fact, I believed I was above the whole experience. I had worked for a human rights organization, done research in Bahrain, gone to an elite graduate school, and was now working for Charlie Rose. I was a fiercely independent, progressively minded woman engaged in important, worldly matters.

Today, I view it differently. I believe that giving it my best at being a hot babe who jumped up and down on behalf of a man with power—a white man in a literal marketplace, no less—could get filed under "EXISTENTIAL." I'd been performing a variation of the act most of my life, exhausting myself trying to look and behave in ways stipulated and rewarded by my culture. We are all multifaceted people with many parts to play. But my most inescapable role had always been one scripted by the patriarchy, in which I blithely safeguarded my society's sexist and racist norms. The part had become so automatic, I didn't even know I was playing it—even as I forged ahead with a life on my own, wanted terms.

As women, we steadfastly march to narratives that keep our own subordination and broader systems of injustice in place. Day in and day out, we devote our time, energy, and creativity to meeting metrics set by the patriarchy, overlooking the cumulative impact of all our drudgery. "There's been a focus—and a right focus—on what men do to women," said the French feminist philosopher Manon Garcia about women's societal subjugation. "But I think it's very important to look at what women do in this, and to have a perspective on their agency . . . We take submission to be passive. Whereas, actually, to submit to man is to do a lot of things—and it's a lot of work."[1] We need to take a hard look at some of what that work entails, especially for white women.

"Good Fit"

White women have been rightly called the foot soldiers of the patriarchy. Historically, we've always upheld social injustice and have always been a threat to non-whites.[2] There's our long-overlooked role as active slave owners, our participation in the Klan, and our history of making false assault allegations resulting in the lynching of untold numbers of innocent Black men. More recently, there's our record of putting racist, misogynistic, homophobic, anti-choice white men into public office, our storming of the Capitol building, and our unwavering support of conspiracy theories that endanger our democracy. And lest we forget our unchecked, sometimes rabid privilege, we will always have Karen memes to show us white women reaching new depths of bigotry and self-entitlement.

But well beyond what is a matter of record, there's also what this book focuses on: the unwitting gap between who we believe ourselves to be and the reality of our actions, and *that* is where the complicity of white women—be they conservative, progressive, country bumpkin, coastal elite, anarchist, or Wiccan—is at its most insidious.* We may not personally be a Karen insofar as we've never

---

* For an extensive historical and contemporary analysis of white women's role in maintaining white supremacy, there are many exceptional reads, including Koa Beck's 2021 book, *White Feminism: From the Suffragettes to Influencers and Who They Leave Behind.* What's addressed in the following pages here is not an attempt to account for the full scope of white women's complicity in its various manifestations.

verbally assaulted Muslim women in a Target parking lot, nor have we called the cops on Black people for swimming in the pool of their own apartment complex. But what we *have* done is something that's actually far more sinister and difficult to confront: we've crafted our sense of self from the cultural narratives that surround us—more specifically, white supremacist patriarchal narratives in which we are the celebrated, uncontested norm of femininity. Inherent to our own protagonism is our status above women of color, and it's a status to which we remain willfully blind.

If you're a white woman like me, you've been given ample opportunity in recent years to reflect on systemic racism and how you're implicated. But as with every topic addressed in this book, there is a difference between knowing and truly understanding. As I set out in solicitation of mea culpas from my white peers, I found that we still struggle to articulate specifics on how we uphold the patriarchy. We know that our role is undeniable, we have contrition, we say that we must do better, and yet we remain vague on what *specifically* we have done. This would come as no surprise to one of the most prominent voices to emerge in recent years on the subject of white people's racism, the bestselling author and educator Robin DiAngelo. She informs progressives like me about their "white fragility"—about how hard it is for us to acknowledge with honest self-awareness that we might actually be . . . a bit racist. When it comes to difficult conversations about racism and injustice, we're more interested in protecting our ideal sense of self than doing the difficult work of recognizing how our own thinking and behavior can be problematic. We deflect, sometimes with tears, criticism back at those people of color willing to speak honestly about how our actions have affected them.

We can intellectualize all we want the truth that some people get ahead because of their whiteness while still opting for a narrative that makes systemic injustice inapplicable to us personally. We can tell ourselves that we're good people who are playing the game meritocratically. And that very well might be true, to an extent—but in no way does it disqualify us from being complicit in the system at large. In no way does it negate our white privilege, nor does it change the reality for non-whites.

For all my professional life, time and again, people in relatively powerful positions have thought I was a "good fit." When I began at *Charlie Rose*, the executive producer thought I was a "good fit." It was not Charlie's style to let anyone feel too confident, but he also once said he thought I "might" be a "good fit." When I interviewed for my next job as a corporate speechwriter, I was told I would be a "good fit" with many of the clients the firm had on retainer—and that I was "very presentable." Being a good fit gives one a sense of assurance and belonging that ironically affirms what we think about ourselves—our distinct, individual character. It is simultaneously both commendable and out of one's own control.

Whiteness is our society's default racial identity, which grants white women the creative license, indeed the privilege, to be unique individuals—unlike Black women, Latino women, Asian women, and other women of color, who are lumped together and depicted in broad, general terms. Professor of sociology at Hunter College Jessie Daniels writes about white women's inability to acknowledge their own whiteness in her book *Nice White Ladies: The Truth About White Supremacy, Our Role in It, and How We Can Help Dismantle It*. Daniels explains that it's precisely white women's sense of individuality that enables them to deflect difficult truths. Multiple times after delivering talks on white womanhood, Daniels has been approached by white women with explanations as to why her subject matter is inapplicable to them personally. "'I'm not really white; I'm European,' is an actual thing that someone has said to me," she writes. "It's this claim to individuality that is one of the main ways that we try to evade understanding our role in white supremacy."[3]

"As a white woman, I now definitely realize that [Charlie's] sexism played to my advantage in a racist way," a former colleague from the show told me, explaining that this understanding was far from immediate. "It was difficult for me, because admitting the racism felt like I was willingly acknowledging that I *wanted* to be harassed—like I *wanted* to play into that system." She recounted starting out as an intern and competing for a job opening with another female intern who had begun at the same time, who was certainly equally if not more qualified for the position, and who was Black. "Years later I could acknowledge that I got the job because I fit Charlie's idea of who should work there more than she did. Just like how being someone who Charlie might consider attractive felt like part of the hiring criteria."

In acknowledging both attractiveness and whiteness as job qualifications, she was also acknowledging whiteness as our cultural norm for beauty—a standard with implications too profound to overstate. The writer and sociologist Tressie McMillan Cottom informs us that beauty isn't actually what somebody looks like. Beauty is both capital and power. It's used to enforce existing social strata, to exclude, and to render Black women unattractive. Sure, we can all think of Black women so gorgeous that they've been bestowed divine status in our society, but they are few in number, and as Cottom writes: "Any system of oppression must allow exceptions to validate itself as meritorious."[4]

When Cottom wrote an essay in 2013 about Miley Cyrus's

performance twerking with and slapping the bottoms of full-figured Black dancers at the MTV Video Music Awards, she used her own experience with racism and beauty to inform readers about the bodies of Black women—Black women who don't look like Beyoncé, Rihanna, or Halle Berry. Rather, Black women who look like Cottom, who describes herself as "not beautiful." She shares her experience of being harassed by drunk white men and women at bars and other locales: "Women asking to feel my breasts in the ladies' restroom. Men asking me for a threesome as a drunk girlfriend or wife looks on smiling. Frat boys offering me cash to 'motorboat' my cleavage. Country boys in cowboy hats attempting to impress their buddies by grinding on my ass to an Outkast music set." As Cottom explains about Cyrus, the dancers with whom she performed had bodies similar to her own Black body, which means that they were there to accentuate the white superiority of Cyrus's sexuality. "Consider it the racialized pop culture version of a bride insisting that all of her bridesmaids be hideously clothed on her wedding day."[5]

The response white women had to Cottom's argument was as informative as her essay. They wrote to her emphatically insisting that she *was* beautiful, cute as a button and worthy of self-love. Cottom, however, would have none of it. As she later wrote about these women in her book *Thick: And Other Essays*, "They offered me neoliberal self-help nonsense that borders on the religious. They need me to believe beauty is both achievable and individual, because the alternative makes them vulnerable. If you did not earn beauty, never had the real power to reject it, then you are as much a vulnerable subject as I am in your own way."[6] When we define beauty as something meritocratic and within anyone's reach, we white women don't have to question how exactly the patriarchy has advantaged us. And we certainly don't have to question the reality confronted by women of color and all the ways that the norm of our white femininity and the celebration of our beauty have compromised their safety and psychological well-being. This includes the greater rates at which Black women are sexually harassed and assaulted, the fact that they are three times more likely to die in pregnancy than their white peers, and that they are two and a half times more likely to be murdered by a man.[7]

Black women also endure higher rates of humiliation, name-calling, and coercive control—a reality of many workplaces.[8] A 2020 study looked at how Black women experience the white gaze in their professional lives by analyzing more than a thousand tweets containing the hashtag #BlackWomenAtWork. The tweets were originally solicited in March 2017 by the Black activist and podcaster Brittany Packnett after two high-profile Black women had been chastised by white men on the same day on national television: Congresswoman Maxine Waters for her hair and veteran White House correspondent April Ryan for shaking her head in disagreement with Trump's press secretary. Packnett wanted more people to understand how commonplace this kind of mistreatment was and took to X to encourage Black women to share their own similar experiences at work. Researchers, explaining that the power of whiteness is omnipresent yet often invisible in our professional organizations, used the hashtag to map out and categorize the ways in which Black women's bodies and mannerisms are vilified and scrutinized, be it their hair, lips, speech, emotional expressions, or perceived body strength. Their individuality, presence, and ideas go unrecognized, while their stamina is often assumed and exploited as that of "superwoman" or "mammy" who is expected to work harder than her colleagues. Researchers argued that whiteness was imposed, presumed, venerated, and sometimes forced upon Black

female employees, who endured "forms of surveillance, mistreatment, marginalization, and scrutiny" not experienced by their white
peers.[9]

When Rebecca Carroll, a Black author and New York Public
Radio producer, was starting her career in 1997, Charlie hired her
in what she describes as a favor to one of her academic mentors,
Harvard's Henry Louis Gates Jr. She writes in her memoir, *Surviving
the White Gaze*, that upon first meeting with Charlie, over drinks at
a bar, he emphasized that she did not fit the office's mold. "You're
different," he told her. "I like that."[10] In her two years working at
the show, Charlie would belittle Carroll's work in front of staff and
frequently accuse her of pushing her own agenda when she pitched
Black guests. When assigned a panel discussion on Steven Spielberg's
movie *Amistad*, she proposed that, in lieu of the more traditional
interview about making the movie, Charlie question the telling
of slave history through a white lens. He found the suggestion so
off-putting that he made a demonstration by canceling the segment.
Days passed before Carroll was assigned work again. Whenever she
sought to clarify, explore, or question anything related to race, she
was punished.

In the aftermath of Charlie's #MeToo downfall, Carroll wrote
in *Esquire* that, however momentous our cultural examination of
powerful white men might seem, we still weren't talking about the
ramifications for Black women or #MeToo's broader connection
to systemic racism. As she explained: "These are micro-fiefdoms
where white men make the decisions, shape the narrative, and
double down on their delusions of unassailability. At the core of
these delusions is the self-indulged freedom to pursue the epitome
of envy. For white men, that means not just being the richest, most
powerful person in the room—but also preying upon and ultimately

capturing the most desirable woman in the room, too. In America, the most desirable woman in the room—the most sacred, coveted, enshrined woman—has always been the white woman."[11] Carroll is in no way lamenting the fact that Charlie never sexually preyed upon her. Rather, she is explaining that in an office where power dynamics were both gendered and racialized, she did not register; her work, her voice, and her presence were disregarded.

Now contrast Carroll's erasure with my performativeness. Like her, I wanted to succeed at an esteemed media institution. But unlike her, I had scripts with which I could engage the powerful white man—and I followed them. Even as things weren't going as I had planned, I wielded these scripts for a sense of control; I sought to be pleasing and to use my sex appeal for a sense of control. At a very basic level I was both a victim *and* a collaborator, because regardless of my circumstances or my intentions, I still played the part as the patriarchy had scripted it for me. To be clear, I'm confident that Charlie also behaved lecherously toward many women of color, and that women of all backgrounds can seek to be pleasing in moments where they're vulnerable. The point, however, is about what white women do with their proximity to patriarchal power and how we're conditioned to respond to misbehaving white men. Conscious of it or not, we reflexively protect their power and seek to please them because our very own protagonism relies on it.

Polly Young-Eisendrath is a Jungian psychologist who believes that women too often derive their sense of power not from their own actions but from an image created to satisfy men. Her book *Women and Desire: Beyond Wanting to Be Wanted* is about women in general, but I believe that her arguments might be most applicable to white women who have internalized their own femininity as the default femininity. Young-Eisendrath explains that the image of a pleasing, desire-awakening young woman is so potent, and so fundamental to our culture, that it compels women to pursue being desired at the cost of their own identity and individual potential. "We have been culturally programmed so thoroughly to tune in to the subtleties of whether or not we are having the 'desired effect' that we fail to tune in to what we really want or to see how strongly we are motivated by wanting to be wanted," writes Young-Eisendrath.[12] She shares stories of her female patients, who exhaust themselves enacting the image of who they believe they need to be, and whose personal and professional lives reflect an intractable belief that legitimate power can only come from the eyes of their beholders.

There's reason to assume that the compulsion about which Young-Eisendrath writes is all the more consuming when you're the cultural benchmark for what exactly is wanted. As white women, we organize our lives around principles of romantic love rather than autonomy and independence. We focus on the social status and financial security that come from marriage instead of questioning the alternatives for how we might want to live and give of ourselves.[13] Psychologists tell us that women's fantasies about marriage and love have a direct impact on their own pursuit of power. The more we believe that we can find a Prince Charming, the less we care about our own ambitions.[14] A 2022 McKinsey report on women in the workplace indicated that women of color are more ambitious than their white peers despite receiving less support at work. Forty-one percent of them aim to be top executives, in comparison to 27 percent of white women.[15]

When I was deciding where to apply to college, my mother told me to think about the kind of husband I wanted and where he might go to school. That advice rubs me the same way today that it did back then: obnoxiously crass but highly practical—for a white woman, anyway. In 1999, my junior year of college, a sociological study was published titled "Getting a Man or Getting Ahead" that examined the differences between the objectives of white and Black sorority sisters. Whereas the activities of white sororities were organized around finding romantic partnerships, Black sororities were structured to facilitate economic self-sufficiency and help better their communities. Researchers posited that for these sisters, "the modern reality of Black female marriage and poverty rates have shaped the sorority structure."[16] With no guarantee of economic security through finding a partner, Black women focus on self-reliance—while white women can fall back on the patriarchy.

Firmly grounded in reality and lacking fairy tales to aspire to, the resiliency and fortitude of Black women is a staple of America's social and political life—one that's been increasingly acknowledged in recent years with social media rally cries like "Black women will save us!" and "Listen to Black women!" But when we depict Black women as a superhuman monolith, we remain only more likely to perceive their oppression as part of the natural order, and to deny them solutions to the systemic injustices they face on a daily basis.[17] "I think we should all shut the hell up about Black women, and just start fighting for them" is what a forty-four-year-old white woman who works in social justice philanthropy told me. "And I don't say that out of white guilt. I say it because it would actually solve some things."

Workhorses and Show Ponies

An earlier draft of the first *Washington Post* exposé on Charlie Rose's misconduct quoted a source who had told investigative reporter Irin Carmon: "We would say around the office, 'Charlie hires workhorses and show ponies. Who are you going to be?'" This remark was eventually cut from the piece, and although I had never heard it, I was gutted when Carmon shared it. As an intern and later a producer, I had felt the imperative to prove myself a workhorse—and I believed that I had succeeded, judging by the sheer quantity of hours I spent in the office. But what I had never acknowledged to myself—not until I heard the quote, anyway—was that I had actually wanted to be a special kind of workhorse: one that *could* have competed as a show pony but chose not to. In fact, I had invested precious disposable income and free time into honing my show pony aptitudes. That I had never considered this fact relevant to my identity was because I had never felt there was an alternative.

Every day I was working my hardest, putting my best, most independently minded, intelligent self forward. But I was doing so within a culture that had muddled my empowerment with my own objectification. Because that's the message we get from our neoliberal, individualistic patriarchy: everything is attainable and you are perfectible, and perfectibility means being a workhorse *and* a show pony; it means exhausting and depleting ourselves according to market metrics *and* the male gaze; it means striving and then striving even harder to achieve, while becoming so singularly fixated on what we want that we fail to question why and to whose benefit we ever came to want it in the first place. In the end, we're left with neither the energy nor the attention span to challenge the patriarchy.

"I remember thinking, *I need to be dressing up.* Like, *I need to be wearing dresses, and specifically short dresses,*" a former colleague named Anna told me, confessing that it didn't take her long to understand that her professional advancement required that she be physically pleasing to Charlie. After all, she explained, the young women on staff who were extended the most exciting professional opportunities were always the highly attractive ones. Anna was quick to clarify that she never wanted to solicit anything inappropriate from him, merely that looking good was an imperative—and one she didn't question. She took to wearing stilettos, which she falsely insisted were comfortable to colleagues curious about the change in footwear since her arrival at the show. These were shoes in which she would sometimes experience a fifteen-hour workday, occasionally traversing multiple expansive floors of the Bloomberg Tower and, if she had time to risk it, running down the block to Sephora to apply free makeup samples before Charlie came into the office for taping that night. Living in New York on a salary of $25,000 a year in the mid-2000s left her with little money to actually buy makeup or to get the blond highlights that she became fixated on needing.

"Highlights in the city cost, like, three hundred dollars, and I had no money," Anna recalled. "But I remember talking with my mom about it and explaining to her that I really thought getting highlights would help. And she was like, 'Okay . . . Yeah?'" The investment appeared quick to pay off. Her first day with the new locks, a veteran female producer complimented her hair, adding that it was a "wise move" with the boss. That same week Charlie paused while en route to the studio for taping to tell her that she looked nice. While remembering the moment, she laughed in shocked dismay: "It might have been the most validated I felt my whole time working for him, and it had nothing to do with my actual work." As a researcher and before that an intern, Anna had proven herself whip-smart and, equally as important in our office, absolutely hilarious. Yet she'd internalized a certain standard of physical appearance as a precondition for the job—and for her success.

She's not alone. On average, women in the United States dedicate two full weeks a year to their daily beauty maintenance routine and apply some eight dollars' worth of skin care and cosmetic products daily, with women in New York averaging three dollars more, or $300,000 over the course of their lifetime.[18] To be real: self-care is important, even critical. Things like exercise, diet, hair maintenance, and skin care routines add to our well-being and boost our self-confidence. But the male gaze complicates the question: On whose behalf do we work so hard?

During the 1990s, the British sociologist Angela McRobbie became alarmed by cultural changes she was noticing in young women's lifestyle habits concerning consumerism, fashion, and beauty. After prior decades of feminist progress and women becoming more visible, consequential players in public and private institutions, no longer could we categorically say that women didn't have a seat at the table. But as many of the conventional indicators of sexism and inequality faded from view, something else had emerged that McRobbie explains was much harder to pin down: neoliberal narratives about women's choices and empowerment that stemmed from traditional ideals of femininity as well as women's own hypersexualized image. Powerful women exercised powerful libidos, wore powerful lingerie, and delighted in maintaining a powerfully sexy and adequately accessorized wardrobe. According to McRobbie, our consumer culture and our fashion and beauty complex were doing a more effective job, or certainly a more insidious job, at keeping women in check than what we think of as traditional patriarchal repression. "Nobody can say, 'Well, it's the fault of men,' . . . because actually the young women seem to be *choosing* to impose this kind of structure of perfection, of body consciousness, of doing it for themselves," McRobbie explains.[19]

By the 1990s we had culturally made two collective assumptions:

One, feminism had done its work on behalf of gender equality and was no longer needed. Two, we were all enlightened, indeed progressive enough to understand a joke—and, now that society wasn't actually sexist, the humor in our media and entertainment could safely include the sexual objectification of women. Take for example an iconic 1994 Wonderbra ad showcasing the supermodel Eva Herzigová looking down in surprised delight at her breasts that are cupped and pushed up by black lace. "HELLO BOYS," reads the text. In an earlier bygone era this ad might be labeled sexist, but not in the mid-'90s. Feminist author Andi Zeisler offers what she imagines as the ad team's concept review: "This would *seem* sexist if we didn't know better, but we do know better, and because women *know* we know better, this is, in fact, empowering."[20]

Crucial to that message of empowerment is Herzigová's own elation and the sheer joy she manifests from having gorgeous breasts. It's a kind of attitude and exhibitionism that comes with being a show pony. Because if we're not enjoying this whole modern womanhood thing—if we're not deriving immense pleasure from our sex appeal and our sexual agency—it means we're not actually succeeding. That much is clear. But what's not always clear about our quest for sexual empowerment is whether we're bothering to delineate between the male narrative of what gives us pleasure and what *actually* gives us pleasure.

In 2006, I went out for beers with a Serbian friend and three of his buddies: a fellow Serb, an Argentine, and a Spaniard, all of whom had come to the United States for their graduate studies at the University of New Mexico. Conversation among them became animated as they recalled with uproarious amusement their earlier days as PhD students, new to the country and its social mores. At one point the Spaniard raised his hands in demand of the table's silence before declaring: "Before moving to America, never *ever* did I know that I was so good at fucking!" The other three men fell off their stools in laughter, and for the first time that night I interjected, wanting to understand what was so funny. My Serbian friend told me in a tone used to state the obvious: "American women love to fake orgasms." He proudly added that no Serbian woman he knew cared to such an extent about her man's ego.

His declaration, at least as it concerned those of us in the United States, aligns with studies revealing that at least half of heterosexual women report frequently faking it.* As for the percentage of heterosexual women who regularly climax during sex with their male partner, the numbers vary but always seriously lag behind men. One study went so far as to put the orgasm gap between women and men at 39 percent and 91 percent, respectively.[21] These figures speak not only to an inequality of pleasure but to women's willingness to pretend otherwise—to be inauthentic for the sake of the narrative.

Of course, our performative inclinations extend beyond the bedroom—a fact that many of my Gen X peers and I have been reckoning with. Something began unsettling us prior to the #MeToo movement, even prior to Donald Trump's 2016 candidacy. For some of us, having children had forced us to migrate—geographically as well as socially and psychologically—to a place that put into perspective a certain cruelty and disingenuousness of our younger years. All that freedom, time, and energy we spent trying to please. All that compromising of our potential. Professionally speaking, a little

---

* I looked, but cross-country comparisons concerning the heterosexual orgasm gap are a bit tricky. This is partly because women in different countries report faking their orgasms for different reasons. For example, whereas American women might want to boost their partner's ego, women in France allege wanting to wrap things up so they can get to sleep.

submissiveness or sexual objectification had felt a small, perhaps even unnoticeable price for entrance when we had accepted the alternative as exclusion. But now here we were, and not all of us could say that things had worked out as we'd expected. As one Gen Xer told me about her own professional stagnation and economic insecurity: "Well, fuck if I'm not a cliché. This is not the way it was supposed to go. This is *not* what we were told."

Nobody is better versed in the struggles of Gen X women than the author Ada Calhoun, who explores the topic in her book *Why We Can't Sleep: Women's New Midlife Crisis*. We've been working full-time while our kids still live at home, while having less wealth than our parents had at the same age, while said parents are now needing elder care, while being told to lean in, while perimenopause starts bearing down. And if that wasn't enough, many of us now confront a painful chasm between the ideal we had fostered for our lives and the reality we now live. While the concept of a woman "having it all" emerged with the boomers before us, Calhoun writes that it became a mainstream expectation by the time we arrived: "Gen Xers entered life with 'having it all' not as a bright new option, but as a mandatory social condition."[22] The impossible standards and conflicting expectations that had shaped our adolescence went on to pound us in adulthood. Calhoun told me of events on her book tour that turned unexpectedly into highly emotional, consciousness-raising events: "Women would stand up and just start crying. They'd tell me how tired and broken they were."

Adding insult to injury, we Gen Xers are also now the age when we get to personally experience our culture's treatment of older women. Aging sucks for women—there's no other way to put it. Rather than rejoicing in becoming less sexually objectified, I sometimes fear that I've become obsolete. My past few years have been spent in intense examination of what constitutes true female empowerment, reflecting on my own cultural conditioning and submissiveness to men, and the potential it deprived me of. There are days when I am enraged by the cruelty and ridiculous masquerade of it all. And yet, on those same days I will be depressed about my hair, and how much thinner it's gotten. While typing about the patriarchy, I get distracted by my fingernails, how they're no longer strong and smooth but ridged and brittle—and in desperate need of a manicure. Other aspects of aging are less nuanced, like the purple "scribbles" my six-year-old pointed to on my thighs, assuming I had made them with a ballpoint pen. I told him emphatically that they're a normal part of a woman's body while silently wondering if I could afford their removal at the same medical center my old neighbor recommends for Botox. Still, even now, I cannot claim to have sufficiently extricated myself from the burdening sensation that to have lost my youthful appeal is to have lost a role. I cannot find the faith—nor embrace the absolute freedom that would come with it—to not give a fuck.

"Symbolic annihilation" is the term used by media scholars to describe the elimination of select individuals in popular culture, such as people of color, sexual minorities, or the economically disadvantaged. The concept speaks to how media's treatment of groups of people can lead to their erasure from public consciousness, invalidating their very social existence.[23] Symbolic annihilation is what a woman comes to feel when she becomes middle-aged and has been written out of our patriarchal narratives.

Adult women protagonists are rare, and female characters are seldomly featured prominently or positively past the age of thirty-five. The author and film critic Carina Chocano warns how this cuts women off from their future selves. "Most stories are focused on the happy ending, which is supposed to happen in your twenties—as though that's the end of your life, the end of your adventure," she explains. "We are never shown a symbolic path into our own future."[24]

But there's an undeniable upside to getting scraped, which is that we now have less to lose. It's telling that of the first big-name Hollywood actors to voluntarily go on the record against Weinstein within the first couple of weeks of the original *New York Times* exposé, all but two were over thirty-five: Ashley Judd, Rose McGowan, Asia Argento, Mira Sorvino, Gwyneth Paltrow, Angelina Jolie, Rosanna Arquette, and Katherine Kendall—all Gen Xers save for Arquette, who is a boomer. The first well-known actors under thirty-five to accuse the movie mogul of abuse were Lupita Nyong'o, a Black woman of Kenyan and Mexican identity, and the openly pansexual Cara Delevingne, two women for whom Hollywood had never been interested in providing a symbolic path into their own future.

When the patriarchy writes us out, it's time to start rewriting the story.

CHAPTER SIX

Show No Weakness

Among high-profile cases of workplace abuse, the allegations against the legendary movie and theater producer Scott Rudin may be the most extraordinary. Known for his Oscar-nominated movies, such as *Lady Bird*, *The Grand Budapest Hotel*, *The Social Network*, and *No Country for Old Men*, as well as his production of myriad Tony Award–winning plays, Rudin was also known within the industry to be a savagely brutal boss. He is alleged to have ripped computers out of the wall and thrown them at employees' heads, along with telephones, staplers, and glass bowls. He reportedly smashed a monitor down on the hand of an assistant who had failed to get him a seat on a sold-out flight, sending him to urgent care. He is said to have once stepped over the body of an employee who had passed out from sheer exhaustion while ordering to his staff, "I want her gone by the time I get back."[1] When reading about Rudin's abuse, one can't help but wonder how nobody who worked for him *died* in the process—that is, if you don't count the executive assistant who committed suicide about a decade after Rudin pushed him out of a moving car. The assistant's brother doesn't believe that Rudin's abuse alone led him to take his life, but he does believe it was a contributing factor.[2]

When a team of reporters at *New York* magazine interviewed thirty-three of Rudin's former assistants and interns for an exposé on his abuse, some noted that it was precisely *because* of his monstrous reputation that "Scott Rudin Productions" looked so good on a résumé. It was a rite of passage, a sign that someone could succeed in an ultracompetitive industry. "Every interview I've done since then, people bring it up. They're all aware of the reputation of that place and what it means," said one of his former assistants. "I'm embarrassed about the extent to which I wore this whole experience as a badge of honor for years," said a former intern who later worked as a paid reader. "At parties or in classes, or when I was at a meeting in L.A., that was a great point of conversation: 'I survived Scott Rudin's office.' 'Oh, wow. What was that like?' I bragged about it rather than stopping to reflect and say, *No, this is awful. This is not an environment anybody should be asked to work in.*"[3]

Nowhere in the Western canon is someone praised for opting out of painful toil, for tossing their hands up and saying, *Nah, I don't need this.* Rather, our belief in the unlimited potential of every individual as well as the ability of hard work to pay off means that we will want, above all else, to prove ourselves tough. We'll take more pride in having withstood workplace abuse than we would have in trying to actually end it. To have endured it, to have kept our heads down and never once uttered "Mercy," proves we have what it takes. And to do what, exactly? That isn't important. What's important is that we've become the Vin Diesel of our story, and if we're Vin Diesel, then everything is good. *We* are good, because *toughness* is good.

Scott Rudin's office was an extreme, but it was also the perfect distillation of toughness as accolade—our culture's conflation of suffering that is senseless, demeaning, or exploitative with virtues like discipline, ambition, and commitment. This worship of toughness drives our complicity. In a neoliberal, patriarchal society likes ours, professional cruelty and exploitation offer a means to validation and deservedness while disproportionately burdening those with an additional need to prove their place, such as women and people of color. It's a reality made only more severe by the centrality of work to our own identities. We see weakness as nothing less than an existential threat.

Madness, Anxiety, and Utter Exhaustion

My first few months of motherhood were brutal. An emergency caesarean had left me with an internal staph infection, a damaged bladder, and stuck on a regimen of horse-pill-sized antibiotics that gave me both nausea and the sensation of a shattered skull. My son's hourly demand for nursing wasn't helping my recovery, nor was the fact that my husband and I had just moved to a new country where we had no friends or familial support. In desperation, we reached out to an experienced night nurse for help. On her very first visit, she sat with me on our living room sofa and calmly asked me to understand the single, most crucial truth about my situation: "Right now, ninety-nine percent of your problems stem from sleep deprivation."

My first thought should have been a benevolent one that reframed, say, my skills as a mother or the viability of my marriage. Instead, memories surfaced of my encounters with Charlie: how physically and mentally exhausted I had been throughout my experience working for him and how intense and high-stakes every aspect of it felt. It was the first time in years that I had granted him any brain space, likely because I was too weak to keep him out. Two years later, when the #MeToo movement came along, my postpartum struggle would help shape how I came to understand my vulnerability as his employee. I wrote in an essay in 2018 that "perhaps most significant—even more significant than my career aspirations and my dependence on a paycheck—was that Charlie's advances occurred in a professional environment of madness, anxiety, and utter exhaustion. One can function in such an atmosphere for only so long before ceasing to operate at one's best, most lucid self."

There were many for whom this resonated, including Beth Silvers, a Kentucky native and host of the *Pantsuit Politics* podcast. She said that although I was writing about the media industry, my description could apply almost anywhere. Her cohost, Sarah Stewart Holland, described her time working on Capitol Hill: "Who worked the hardest? Who stayed up the latest? Who sacrificed the most? Who hadn't eaten and exercised? *That* was the badge of honor."[4]

There is a physiological component to our vulnerability, whether it's sexual misconduct or other workplace abuse, and it's exacerbated by our belief that a good worker is an *overworked* worker. When we've already ceded our own exploitation as employees, having embraced the long hours, mental overload, and complete personal sacrifice that comes with the job, clarity on what even constitutes abusive behavior falls by the wayside.

To be clear, many people are overextended at work due to their economic insecurity and because they have no choice but to exhaust themselves by laboring strenuously. However, our concern here is something far more voluntary and white-collar. It comes from both a willingness to let our jobs dictate our well-being and a matter of pride when they do. In America, being overworked is a status symbol. We boast about it, because it means that we're in demand.[5] Despite the overwhelming evidence that working too many hours only hurts an employee's productivity and creativity, we're unable to imagine another path to success. "I saw the greatest minds of my generation log 18-hour days—and then boast about #hustle on Instagram," writes Erin Griffith, on the subject of "hustle culture."[6] Or, as Elon Musk gallantly tweeted: "Nobody ever changed the world on 40 hours a week."[7]

The origin of this gluttony for professional punishment traces back to the sixteenth century, with the Reformation and what would become our Protestant work ethic. Later identified by Max Weber as the driving ethos of capitalism, a belief in work as "a calling" and as a way to give thanks to God pushed paid labor to the center of modern society and, by extension, our lives. With the Industrial Revolution came hired, salaried work as we know it, along with new demands for productivity and efficiency.[8] The Protestant aspect of our work ethic has faded, but our devotion to work—and to working hard—has only increased. Today, we Americans spend far more time working than people in other countries of similar size and productivity—working roughly ten weeks more a year than our German counterparts, and about 25 percent more hours a year than those in the Netherlands and Norway.[9]

"For those of us who went to work there, it was like a drug that we could get self-worth from," recalled a former Amazon employee named Dina in a 2015 *New York Times* exposé on the company's culture. She described herself as addicted to the notion of success at the tech giant, once going four days straight without sleep, and increasing her productivity by spending her own money on a freelancer in India to do data entry. When these admissions generated additional press coverage, Dina took to LinkedIn and *Medium* to say that the long hours she put in were "MY CHOICE." She shared her most notable achievements while at Amazon, which she attributed to the company's Leadership Principles, a highly defined list of metrics by which employees are driven and critiqued. "When operating from a place of fear and acute stress that their survival is threatened, humans can do ugly things. Employees are mistreated, talent is stifled, and opportunities are missed," she wrote. "However, when you properly utilize the spirit of these principles, magical things are possible."[10]

Those who have studied the psychology of cults note that recruits will often be deprived of sleep so that their minds are kept in a debilitated state—so that they'll be less likely to question whatever dogma the cult feeds them.[11] Our devotion to work can do the same. The fatigue blurs our judgment and leaves us all the more single-minded on being a good employee—and not necessarily a good person. "The moral mind is not our default mind," the Princeton psychologist John M. Darley tells Margaret Heffernan in *Willful Blindness*. "In a very competitive environment, where you're under a lot of stress, a lot of cognitive load, you won't necessarily even see that there is a moral consideration at all."[12]

Physical and mental exhaustion is more than precariousness; it's often a prerequisite for entry into our most competitive industries and most prestigious institutions. In 2021, a leaked internal survey among thirteen junior analysts at Goldman Sachs showed that they worked an average of ninety-five hours a week and slept an average of five hours a night. All respondents said that their job had negatively impacted their personal relationships, and 77 percent of them claimed to have experienced workplace abuse. "The sleep deprivation, the treatment by senior bankers, the mental and physical stress . . . ," wrote one of the analysts. "I've been through foster care and this is arguably worse."[13]

The leak was rare for an industry in which employees are expected to "man up" and deal. The team of analysts who took and then compiled the survey feedback did so only after the pandemic had exacerbated their working conditions. With the hopes that there could be a modicum of change, they presented the results as a PowerPoint presentation to a senior executive. The bank eventually responded with an offer of higher pay, by which time five of the original thirteen analysts had left, four of them women of color.[14]

It's a cruel irony that those most equipped to prove their professional toughness are often those who have been relatively coddled by life. I was once friends with a man from Ohio who told me about how when he was in his twenties, he landed his first job in private equity, and needed to "really kick ass." To help him do so, he hired a personal assistant for his life outside the office: a young woman who took care of his grocery shopping, dry cleaning, personal calendar—even picked out birthday presents for his parents. All he had to do was focus on work and get to the gym when he could. This man should not be resented for his strategic approach to professional success, nor for the loving, highly supportive white family with means from which he came. But his story illustrates the socioeconomic barriers to success in competitive industries and who the game is designed to favor.

"Masculinity contest culture" is what researchers label a set of workplace values most prevalent in male-dominated, high-stakes, hierarchical industries such as finance, tech, television, and surgery. Such a work culture has four specific attributes: an attitude of "show no weakness"; a reverence for strength and stamina; a commitment to work above all else, even family; and a dog-eat-dog attitude of ruthless competition.[15] Organizations aligned with these values, according a 2018 survey analysis of thousands of workers in the United States and Canada, are where professional misconduct and illegal behavior are most likely to occur. They're also, more often than not, highly dysfunctional workplaces. "At work, this pressure to prove 'I have what it takes' shifts the focus from accomplishing the organization's mission to proving one's masculinity," write researchers. "The result: endless 'mine's bigger than yours' contests." Employees brag about workloads, cut corners, make risky decisions, and refuse ownership of their mistakes. Cooperation, trust, and mental well-being are undercut, while one group of colleagues is suspected of not "having what it takes": women and people of color. They're put in a professional catch-22, in which they must work even harder to prove themselves. Yet when they do, they're frequently reprimanded for displaying the same behaviors of their white male counterparts, such as aggression and self-promotion.[16]

A forty-two-year-old Korean American named Chloe actually thought she had sidestepped these gendered double binds by working for a tech giant, more specifically Amazon. She appreciated being someplace so data-driven, where an employee's closely monitored results would speak for themselves. Chloe was in her late thirties at the time and had never worked so much or so hard in her life. When she had her first child, she submitted a report to her boss five hours before giving birth—on her due date. But even with all the numbers on her performance, she is convinced that the sexism was still there. When, for example, her work was measured according to the company's lauded Leadership Principles—the same values cited by other employees for making "magical things" possible—she felt that gender biases had introduced themselves stealthily. She explained that, despite the speed at which decision-making was demanded of Amazon employees, women were still expected to do things more gracefully than their male counterparts. "Male employees who took charge and got a job done matter-of-factly were celebrated—and then promoted. But if I did the same thing, I was punished based on the employee metric 'earn trust.' It meant that I had failed to diplomatically account for everyone's viewpoints," she told me. "Here I am, an Asian woman who has the hard data on my results, and I'm effectively getting a demerit for *daring* to have the same confidence as my male colleagues. I know it happened to other women, too."

A combination of the stress and frustration that comes from being shut out and devalued, coupled with the smaller likelihood of being promoted, is why women experience far greater rates of burnout than men.[17] And yet, despite the soul-crushing exhaustion, Chloe found it excruciatingly difficult to make the decision to leave her job, and not to judge herself harshly for doing so. "I still felt like I was throwing away something good and that by leaving it meant I was a failure." Even when we know it's in our best interest, opting out doesn't come easily.

Writer and distance runner Lindsay Crouse wrote in the *New York Times* about athletes who become martyrs to grit, describing a race she ran in college despite suffering from a syndrome that made her shins swell up. She had dropped to last place and, despite the inability to feel the movement of her legs—only the painful sensation of burning—she kept going. She fell at the finish line, then stood back up with bloody hands and knees. "Under the floodlights, I told everyone I was fine, then went to wash myself off alone," writes Crouse. "It occurred to me only last year, when I took a long

break from running, that this moment of toughness and perseverance, seared in my mind as a point of pride, accomplished nothing.
I spent years doing things like that. Why was I so afraid to stop?"

Workism

In the seven years that my husband and I have lived in Belgium,
most of the locals we've met have been through our sons, who
are in the public school system. We've befriended other parents at
drop-offs, birthday parties, playdates, and chance encounters at the
playground—all the while chitchatting about our kids, their teachers,
our hobbies, and our vacations. I noticed, though, that one topic was
always conspicuously absent: work. We would know and socialize with
many of these people for years before learning of their professions.

I eventually came around to asking a Belgian friend, by text, if
culturally it was in poor taste to inquire about people's professions.
She wrote that there's absolutely no such taboo and added, along
with a laughing emoji sprouting tears, "It's only because there are
more interesting things to talk about."

Sure, I thought . . . but are there any topics more relevant to
our daily lives? To what consumes us? To who we *are*? Mine was
a typically American reaction insofar as work is central not just to
our lives but to our identities—the single most important means
by which we prove our worth.[18] And when we allow our work to
define so much about our very being, we're not going to let some
mistreatment or questionable behavior get in the way of our professional potential. Not when we're fuckin' Vin Diesel.

Derek Thompson, who covers trends in work, technology, and
culture for the *Atlantic*, writes that, for the college-educated elite
in America, "work has morphed into a religious identity—promising
transcendence and community." Thompson calls this phenomenon

"workism"—a belief that work is not just a necessity of economic production "but also the centerpiece of one's identity and life's purpose." Whereas in most countries poor people work more than wealthy people, beginning in the 1980s this trend reversed itself in the United States. "The highest-earning Americans worked longer and longer hours, in defiance of expectations or common sense," explains Thompson. "In a time of declining religiosity, rich Americans seemed to turn to their career to fill the spiritual vacuum at the center of their life."[19]

Wealthy white men were the first adherents of workism, but it has since spread to women and younger generations. A 2019 Pew Research Center report on the anxieties of U.S. teenagers showed that 95 percent of teens ranked "having a job or career they enjoy" as "extremely or very important"—higher than any other priority, including helping people in need, getting married, or having children.[20] There is certainly no harm in individuals professionally doing what they love and finding a sense of meaning along the way. But when work is so critical to our ideal sense of self, careerism comes into play. We strive for professional advancement with everything we've got, overlooking ethical considerations along the way, sometimes not even mindful that we're doing so.

The moral philosopher Elizabeth Kamarck Minnich builds upon the work of her former mentor Hannah Arendt—well known for her reporting on the trial of Adolf Eichmann and her use of the phrase "the banality of evil"—to examine how the worst, most extensive kinds of harm are carried out by normal people who don't have bad intentions but who are simply acting without critical thought. In her book, aptly titled *The Evil of Banality: On the Life and Death Importance of Thinking*, Minnich writes: "I now believe careerism to be prime among the preparations for extensive evil: it practices and rewards us for playing a game well and in its own terms, absorbing us to such an extent that attentiveness and free thinking can yield entirely to a calculating, analytical intelligence that moves only within the bounds of the game."[21] She provides the example of two men with the German Police Battalion 101 who refused Nazi killing orders. In interviews, both men emphasized their lack of professional ambition. They were older, and one of them had his own side business as a craftsman. "Were they wiser, less swayed by Nazi rhetoric, less prone to passionate causes or murderous fury?" asks Minnich. "No, they simply did not care as much about advancing in their careers."

Careerism fortunately does not manifest itself with the same gravity in modern America as it did in Nazi Germany, but I know from personal experience that it can be as mindlessly self-interested as Minnich warns. When I was younger and more ambitious, my own careerism was like tunnel vision, with too much left to the periphery. In March 2008, Charlie showed up for taping with a horrendous black eye and a bandage above his eyebrow. He told staff that he had tripped over a pothole while crossing Fifty-Ninth Street, leaving us to figure out what kind of contorted fall could possibly leave such a wound. Later that May, my housemate left an alarmed voice mail: he was having drinks with the close friend of a woman who said she had given Charlie the black eye during a physical altercation. The description that my housemate was given of this woman matched that of a prior employee who had worked for and openly dated Charlie. According to staff chatter, the two had broken up acrimoniously earlier that March—the same week of his Midtown misstep. My housemate and I weren't exceptionally close, and he didn't know much about my internship. But he had called me in a state of alarm, after hearing enough that he felt an urgent necessity to warn me that Charlie was a violent man and that I needed to be careful when I was alone with him.

None of the women who went on the record against Charlie maintain that he was violent, and I'll likely never know for sure how he got his eye busted. But I remember very clearly my reaction to the warning: I dismissed it entirely. I was too busy, too taxed out, and had too much on the line. I had been working for free as an intern for Charlie for a year by that point, skipping classes in graduate school to do so, all to finally become a salaried producer with a line on my résumé to match. My hard work and professional aspirations had already been compromised enough by Charlie's behavior, and in that moment I didn't want to know any more than I already knew. He was a handsy, loony, ill-tempered perv, and for my sake that would be the extent of it.

I'd given far too much to my professional pursuit to open myself up to an even uglier story. And if I felt that way, a year into an internship that was landing me a job early in my career, what about the woman who's spent the entirety of her adulthood in pursuit of becoming a cardiac surgeon and finally completed her fifteen years of required medical training? Or the lawyer whose career objective was set when he first cracked open an LSAT prep book, then went $200,000 into law school debt, then landed the prized clerkship, yet still had to rely on a family friend's connections to get his foot in the door at an elite law firm? Or what about pretty much *anyone* who has stayed an exhausting, thankless course on their career path, holding out because they're finally within reach of the job title they believe will justify all the personal sacrifices they've made along the way? Within this larger picture of personal dedication and drudgery, professional misconduct registers as insignificant and certainly not worth the risk of speaking out about. This is how workism becomes more than an ethos: it can be a sunk cost to which we are so firmly anchored that we would never consider stirring the waters.

The #MeToo movement spurred reckonings in some industries more than others. Celebrity and whiteness were often cited as the right ingredients for some amount of accountability: famous men who could command our attention, and white female victims whose voices we could trust. But the movement also took hold in industries with high turnover, for which intensive educational training isn't necessary: entertainment, journalism, politics. These professions also have high crossover with other fields: journalists often find work in corporate communications, political staffers often jump to private consulting, etc.

Another key aspect of the industries in which the movement ignited was passion. These were places full of ambitious entry-level employees who were incredibly passionate about the fields they were in and eager to prove their resiliency. And when someone's perceived as highly devoted to or enthusiastic about their job, their mistreatment is generally more likely to be condoned—as indicated by psychological research into a tendency that's called "passion exploitation." In eight studies covering 2,400 participants in the United States, researchers found that respondents were more toler-ant of someone sacrificing time with family, working on weekends, working unpaid, or taking on demeaning tasks outside their job description if they were employed in social work, the arts, or another field traditionally associated with "passionate" employees. The inverse was also true: if respondents learned of someone being mistreated at work, they were highly inclined to assume that the person was passionate about what they did. Regardless of an employee's feelings, these beliefs only legitimize workplace abuse.[22]

I spoke with the forty-five-year-old director of a global health initiative who had never heard of the term "passion exploitation," but she knew what I meant immediately. "I guess 'passion exploitation' is just part of the only work culture I've ever known." She emphasized to me that when you're trying to do things like deliver lifesaving HIV/AIDS medications to the poorest countries in the world, the unspoken assumption is that whatever personal sacrifice is asked of you, it's worth it. "At my last job, women who had just returned from their unpaid maternity leave were immediately expected to travel to the [Democratic Republic of the Congo] for two weeks, maybe more, never mind that they were still breastfeeding." And when inappropriate behavior happened internally, she indicated that the mission always came first. There were people within the organization doing unquestionably inappropriate things, like a program director sleeping with others on staff and being generally demeaning to female colleagues. But nobody was interested in holding him accountable, given the impact it would have on their work.

When lives are on the line, it's hard to argue that professional misconduct shouldn't take a back seat. For those who suffer the professional misconduct, the workism becomes altruism. To demand their own workplace dignity feels anything but noble. A forty-three-year-old woman in healthcare told me about the years she worked serving low-income families in Boston with vital services, during which time she reported to a department chair whose treatment of a primarily all-female staff included undermining them in meetings, bullying them in private, spreading rumors internally, and taking credit for other people's accomplishments. "I worked with single mothers who struggled to feed their children, so I figured that, by comparison, putting up with a maniacal supervisor wasn't that bad," she said. "It would have been so much easier to say 'Absolutely not' or even leave my position if the work wasn't so important to me."

It's often reported that younger people today are relatively more disillusioned about work, rejecting it as a basis for their personal identity in greater numbers.[23] The youngest in our labor force, Generation Z, have confronted wage stagnation and crushing student loan debt amid growing wealth inequality. Might there be hope for change? Kathi Weeks, professor of feminist studies at Duke University and author of the seminal 2011 book *The Problem with Work*, which questions the dominance work has come to assume in wealthy societies, has her doubts. When asked in 2021 if Covid-19 had ended our obsessive love affair with work, she nodded to the psychological benefits of workism: "Working hard to convince ourselves of our love for work might be a rational adaptation, a tactically brilliant move, even," she said. "The prospect of finding some hope and pleasure in the wastelands of capitalism is always worth the effort. So why not buy into the fantasy?"[24]

"Watch How I Can Put Up with This Stuff"

When I spoke over Zoom with Melanie Nichol, a cultural anthropologist at Oregon State University, she was wearing chunky jewelry and bright red lipstick. She emoted with warmth and dramatic flair, particularly as she talked about social justice, Spanish literature, the folklore class she teaches . . . and her time as a corrections officer in the Springfield Municipal Jail. Reflecting on her experience with a team of mostly male corrections officers, she told me about a defining moment in her indoctrination: the first time she got into an altercation with a fellow officer, ramping her own tone up to match his insolence, and receiving the instant respect of her coworkers for doing so.

"When I saw the admiration from other officers that I was tough—and I gave it right back and I wouldn't complain—that just felt amazing," she told me. "I look back and it's so gross, but the reward was so great."[25] Nichol eventually left her job to go back to school, then to study abroad—experiences that gave her what she described as a healthy distance from corrections. When she eventually returned to Springfield, she took a job as a Spanish-language dispatcher with the local police department, anticipating that it would be a relatively more professional workplace than corrections. But it was a male-dominated office where weakness was deplored and targeted all the same. Colleagues were cruel and abusive, sexual harassment was rampant, and Nichol fell right back into her tough-woman act. "I created the idea that if I was tough and kicked ass, I was breaking out of a gender role and separating myself from weak women," she said. "I was like, *Watch how I can put up with this stuff!*"

For far too many women, pushing past sexism and abuse at work relies on flexing our toughness. Whatever our circumstances, whatever the power dynamics or mistreatment at play, if we can be tough, we can be the heroes of our own stories. *Watch how I can put up with this stuff* is a way to take hold of the narrative—and it's a lot more flattering to our sense of self than some of the alternatives (e.g., *I regularly face inequality and mistreatment and have no adequate or uncostly means of addressing it*).

Surviving professional misconduct or other abusive treatment is an accomplishment we should recognize. No one's struggle should be minimized or forgotten. But framing the experience in terms of our own resiliency can also condone the abuse. In 2022,

the author Laura Lippman spoke out on the *You Are Good* podcast about what she viewed as her fellow boomers' tendency to
romanticize their own professional mistreatment. She reminded
them that their ability to survive and even succeed in abusive
environments didn't make those situations any less wrong. "I still
see women who have a really hard time letting go of the idea that
surviving sexual harassment—just really mean, abusive workplace
cultures—is a badge of honor," she said. "Yay for you. There's no
positive in it. You're not better for that. You're not tougher for
that. You just went through it."[26]

I've heard multiple other female former employees of the *Charlie Rose* show make light of a sexual harassment lawsuit brought
against Charlie by three younger women at CBS. What *they* had
reported experiencing—the touching and the inappropriate sexual
banter—"wasn't even that bad," certainly not in comparison to the
legitimate abuse that *we* experienced. We should support their
cause, the reasoning went, while patting ourselves on the back for
having endured far worse.

A Gen X consultant named Cathy took me back to the moment
she proved her place in the cult of female toughness, a mindset that
would constrain her well into adulthood. She was fifteen years old, at
a backyard party, socializing comfortably from her patio chair. Among
the ten or so other teenagers there was her new love interest, along
with a budding pyromaniac who lit a plastic cup on fire. When someone attempted to put out the flame by kicking the cup, the molten
plastic shot across the patio and hit Cathy, giving her third-degree
burns along the entire side of her right bicep. "I remember thinking,
Be cool. Just slough it off and don't go to the hospital, don't get treatment,"
she said. "It was this feeling as a young woman that nothing can faze
you. Instead of feeling all the feelings, you just have to move through

it." She wrapped her arm in some gauze and stayed at the party until late that evening.

Fast-forward to Cathy's mid-twenties, when she was beginning a job with a consulting firm in Washington, D.C., and an older male client made a sexualized joke about how she looked in the dress that she was wearing at a work dinner. "I can't even remember what specifically he said, or maybe I've blocked it out. I only remember that it took the air out of the room." She left the table and went to the bar, where her boss followed to ask her if she was okay. She was fine, she told him, and played it down—"not to make things less awkward for the harasser," she said, "but to show that I was tough; to say, *This doesn't affect me.*"

This mindset feels compulsory for women and keeps them from getting the support they could use. A thirty-nine-year-old U.S. diplomat named Maya told me that she'd feel like a failure if she had to report a problem with someone at work. "There would definitely be a part of me that felt I should have been able to fix it. Because at the end of the day, if you're tough, you just deal with it." The irony, which she could recognize, is that she said this as someone who had served as her consulate's Equal Employment Opportunity counselor, the person who employees go to for guidance when they feel they've been harassed or discriminated against.

As much as anyone she knew, Maya believed in the critical importance of employee accountability when it came to workplace abuse, but all of that took a back seat to her need to be invulnerable. She spoke of having witnessed "disgusting" behavior among past colleagues that had deeply troubled her, explaining that, in a larger context of long hours and personal sacrifice away from family and home, employees can truly believe that they deserve to commit their transgressions. They *deserve* their drunken binges, their office flings, their sexist humor, and their moments of misdirected fury. Maya figured that if she couldn't take all of it in stride, she wasn't cut out to be in the Foreign Service.

Every work culture is embedded in a larger culture, and the toughness demanded of Maya is symptomatic of a culture that values competition and hyperindividualism. Succeeding often means "playing the game," and for many women that means behaving just as mercilessly as any of their male counterparts. Some feminists argue that an ethos of *Watch how I can put up with this stuff*—or even *Watch how I can dole it out myself*—has become an imperative for women who want to prove their value as human capital. And especially for women both white and white-collar, such moxie can be found through the etiquette of a new kind of self-empowerment: neoliberal feminism.

Coined by Catherine Rottenberg, a professor of feminist theory and culture at the University of London, "neoliberal feminism" is like the "girl power" so many of us were sold in our teens insofar as it touts our empowerment while doing zilch to challenge existing social or institutional hierarchies. It's a kind of feminism that, according to Rottenberg, recognizes gender inequality "while simultaneously denying that socioeconomic and cultural structures shape our lives." Instead, the solutions it posits to things like the wage gap and sexual harassment require that women focus on their own enterprising capacities—to essentially play the game of patriarchal neoliberal capitalism *smarter* and to never cease optimizing their own market value. This message is for a select group only. As Rottenberg explains: "Incessantly inciting women to accept full responsibility for their own well-being and self-care, neoliberal feminism ultimately directs its address to the middle- and upper-middle classes, effectively erasing the vast majority of women from view." Gender equality—if that's what we want to call it—is siphoned off for the upwardly mobile, white, heteronormative women like me.[27] Indeed, what Rottenberg calls "neoliberal feminism" shares an awful lot with what's more commonly referred to simply as "white feminism."

Rottenberg began looking at how feminism was being seized upon in 2013 by corporations that were repackaging their products as empowering to women (what in *this* case is sometimes referred to as "pop feminism" or "market feminism"). From Spanx to Swiffer, cigarettes to energy drinks, the market wanted women to find their independence. At the same time, an increasing number of famous women—the likes of Facebook chief operating officer Sheryl Sandberg, Beyoncé, Emma Watson, Hillary Clinton, Ivanka Trump—began to use the label "feminist," something unthinkable during earlier decades, when women who claimed themselves as such were portrayed as unlovable hellcats if not worse.

Rottenberg points out that although "the f-word" was back, still absent was any mention of long-held feminist vocabulary—terms like "autonomy," "rights," and "liberation." In their place were words like "balance," "happiness," and "leaning in"—a self-help lexicon for the working woman that had mass appeal and marketed solutions ostensibly within every woman's reach. Neoliberal feminism provided nothing short of an Emily Post–type guide to white-collar resiliency. A kind of *Watch how I can manage the exploitations of my job with dignity and grace. Watch how I can optimize the precious free time I have with color-coded Excel spreadsheets. Watch how I can succeed as a working mom in a country void of accessible childcare— thanks to the care work of a woman of color who spends a minimum of twelve hours a day in my home.*

In the politically and socially tumultuous years since #MeToo, there has been a surge of mindfulness that women cannot muscle

their way past systemic inequality. Sandberg's feminist proclamations of "leaning in" have since been heavily criticized for messaging
that smacks of an elitist denial of real problems (not all too different from her proclamations denying Facebook's role in spreading
disinformation and undermining our democracy). But the desire to
take the narrative into our own hands by making it a question of
our own weakness versus strength will always be psychologically
appealing, especially in a neoliberal society where work is paramount to one's own identity.

CHAPTER SEVEN

It's Time We Talk About Narcissism

In October 2014, Canadian celebrity and CBC broadcaster Jian Ghomeshi was said to be paranoid that the *Toronto Star* was about to publish accusations against him involving sexually violent behavior. So he decided to get ahead of the story by calling a meeting with CBC executives, to whom he explained that he had been with women who sometimes liked it rough and that any physical harm he'd ever inflicted upon them during sex had been entirely consensual. Ghomeshi reportedly showed his superiors photos of a woman's bruised and cracked rib, along with graphic video footage of his committing sexual violence. To further hammer home that he only provided what these women had wanted of him, he then shared lewd text messages that he'd exchanged with them . . . on his company phone.[1]

It turned out that the *Toronto Star* had actually nixed the story on Ghomeshi due to what was believed to be a lack of corroboration. But with the documentation he had just provided, that would change: CBC executives, deeply alarmed, were forced to take action. Ghomeshi's contract was quickly terminated, sparking public intrigue and precisely the press coverage he had feared.[2] Also made public were allegations of abusive treatment made by his employees, who described his wild fluctuations in temperament as he had demeaned and harassed them. I believe that if Ghomeshi thought he could actually convince higher-ups of his consensual engagement in "a mild form of 'Fifty Shades of Grey'" (as he described it to his followers on social media), it was because he'd been given a pass to brazenly abuse people at the CBC for more than seven years. As the celebrated voice of Canada and the network's golden boy, he'd been a myth too powerful to stop. Whether Ghomeshi truly thought of himself as a morally righteous guy or whether he simply felt entitled to act as he pleased, his self-delusion was the perfect illustration of the wrecking-ball force of male narcissism in our workplaces.

Every one of us gets by with a dollop of self-delusion. The complicity that we're concerned with is, after all, found in the difference between who we like to believe ourselves to be and the actuality of our behavior. But this difference is much greater for a narcissist. The gap between the narcissist's real and his ideal self is so big that the rest of us get stuck precariously treading in its absurdity, losing our own bearings as we do. One of Ghomeshi's former producers, Rachel Matlow, told me that it was impossible to pinpoint a single moment at which his cruelty had become normalized. Rather, he had always overpowered his staff's ability to reason clearly or to understand what they were compromising of themselves. Matlow likened the psychological experience of working for him to being a frog boiled alive—"one degree at a time."[3]

As for the meeting at which Ghomeshi showed network

executives video footage of his own sexual violence, Matlow said it was the perfect encapsulation of their former boss: "A narcissist can't help but think they have the power to drive not just the narrative but the reality."

That resonated with me, and coincided with the stories of so many others who had struggled to cope with the delusions of powerful men—men who *had* driven the narrative, be it with their temper, dishonesty, denial, gaslighting, manipulativeness, impulsiveness, divisiveness, vindictiveness, shrewdness, or even the ability to inspire pity on their own forlorn behalf. They were emotionally unstable and wrought chaos wherever they went, yet they were unstoppable. In fact, they had come out on top because our systems rewarded their arrogance and treated their sense of privilege as canon, and because brilliant men, our logic goes, are too busy being brilliant to give a fuck about conventional mores or what the average dolt might think. As one of Harvey Weinstein's former assistants said about his tendency to wander around naked while giving his dictation: "You think, *Oh, that's okay. He's far too important to wear trousers.*"[4]

These are individuals who could be called a lot of things—assholes, jerks, lechers, blowhards, bastards, raging lunatics, grandiose pricks, or dangerously insecure. Or they could more tactfully be called "entitled," a word that steers clearer of presumptions about mental health for which I have neither the medical credentials nor the firsthand clinical insight to be making. Yet I choose to call these men narcissists because I believe it more precisely speaks to the problem at hand: our own vulnerability—individually, institutionally, and culturally—to an extreme level of male self-aggrandizement. Narcissism reveals as much about us and our neoliberal, celebrity-driven, patriarchal society as it does the men in question.

Certainly not every sexual harasser or abusive boss is a narcissist. (Nor, for that matter, is every narcissist a sexual harasser or an abusive boss.) But time and again the traits I heard people use to describe destructive male superiors in their workplaces fit the picture of narcissistic abuse—one I knew all too well having worked for Charlie. By putting us in fear mode and constantly changing the narrative, narcissistic male bosses undermine our ability to respond with clearheaded reason. Along the way, as we struggle to keep pace, our loyalty is extracted as the terms of engagement.

One might wonder: Aren't women also narcissists? They most certainly are. Many women are up there among the most egomaniacal of bosses. But in a patriarchal world that scripts him as "the Subject" and her as "the Other," narcissistic women ascend the ranks despite their egocentrism, whereas narcissistic men are able to do so in large part because of it—because their self-delusions are pulled directly from our narratives of male greatness. Boys grow up seeing authoritative, self-assured men rule the world, while girls grow up being punished for displaying aggressiveness or assertiveness. This cultural reality fuels a rate of narcissism in men that is roughly 40 percent higher than in women, a gender disparity that ranks among the highest of any psychological attribute.[5]

A note of caution, however, as we are wading into a subject area that for all its popular usage often remains misunderstood. Narcissism is a universal aspect of human psychology that manifests itself along a continuum—and understanding it as such can help us to avoid categorical pitfalls about a subject that is far from uniform. We all exhibit a narcissistic trait or two from time to time. In fact, sometimes a bit of narcissism is helpful in generating the confidence we need to get shit done. If someone exhibits such traits most of the time, they fall further down the continuum and can be described as having a narcissistic personality—that is, one characterized by a lack of empathy and an inflated sense of self-importance. At the tail end of the spectrum are those who suffer from full-fledged narcissistic personality disorder, which can be diagnosed only by a medical professional who would assess whether the patient in question meets a sufficient number of criteria listed for NPD in the *Diagnostic and Statistical Manual of Mental Disorders*, more commonly referred to as the *DSM.* * While estimates vary, it's believed that .5 to 5 percent of the general population have NPD.[6]

What follows is not an attempt to make armchair diagnoses involving a mental disorder. I leave that to the professionals. Rather, I'm using the terms "narcissist" and "narcissistic" as the most truthful descriptors I have to categorize a specific brand of brute power that is wreaking havoc in our workplaces and beyond.

---

* The diagnostic criteria in the *DSM-5-TR*, the most current version of the *DSM* at the time of writing, reads as follows: A pervasive pattern of grandiosity (in fantasy and behavior), a need for admiration, and lack of empathy, beginning by early adulthood and present in a variety of contexts, as indicated by five (or more) of the following:

1. Has a grandiose sense of self-importance (e.g., exaggerates achievements and talents, expects to be recognized as superior without commensurate achievements).
2. Is preoccupied with fantasies of unlimited success, power, brilliance, beauty, or ideal love.
3. Believes that he or she is "special" and unique and can only be understood by, or should associate with, other special or high-status people (or institutions).
4. Requires excessive admiration.
5. Has a sense of entitlement (i.e., unreasonable expectations of especially favorable treatment or automatic compliance with his or her expectations).
6. Is interpersonally exploitative (i.e., takes advantage of others to achieve his or her own ends).
7. Lacks empathy: is unwilling to recognize or identify with the feelings and needs of others.
8. Is often envious of others or believes that others are envious of him or her.
9. Shows arrogant, haughty behaviors or attitudes.

"Did He Know How Bad He Was?"

In my conversations with Charlie's former employees, one question came up more than a few times and always with sincere wonderment: "Did he know how bad he was?" they would ask. Inherent to this question was the acknowledgment that Charlie's version of events—indeed, his perception of the world—didn't always seem tethered to reality. One longtime producer had wanted to assume that yes, he did know. "He wouldn't have kept some things secret if he didn't think his behavior was inappropriate," she said before immediately changing her mind—twice. She had worked for Charlie for more than ten years and still couldn't decide.

While we all create our own sense of self selectively, editing our stories in ways that keep us comfortably blind to less flattering realities, narcissists do so with far greater license—especially when confronted by facts that challenge their ideal self-image. It's impossible to answer the question of whether Charlie knew because if he ever did come to understand that he was comporting himself in lecherous, abusive ways, his newfound awareness was likely short-lived. He could edit away his own realization, either deleting it from his mind entirely or forging a new story that vindicated his behavior.

What makes working for a narcissist so destabilizing, beyond their rage, is that they don't just take hold of the narrative; they never cease redrafting it to their advantage. It's precisely what made Charlie a juggernaut of male entitlement. He would shower praise upon an employee about a segment they produced and then turn around and viciously berate them about that same segment the very next day. He would boisterously announce raises at a staff holiday party, then neither implement nor mention them ever again. He would call at 5:30 a.m. to delight in sharing the sexual fantasy in which you were featured and that afternoon speak threateningly to you about the importance of the segment you were producing. He could swing instantly and unabashedly between effusive jollity and explosive anger, and surviving as his employee meant knowing at all times where to be vis-à-vis the swing of his mood pendulum. It was mentally, emotionally, and physically depleting. Because when the person at the top is unaccountable to reason, or even to what they said forty-five minutes earlier, the only thing you can do is try to keep up.

Along the way, one becomes inclined to treat each moment with the same dismissiveness that the narcissist does, losing the inclination to question the morality or logic of their own behavior. If Charlie wasn't bound to reality, did that mean any of us had to be? As for me personally, maybe I didn't have to account for the emails that I sent him chock-full of the sycophancy I knew he liked. Maybe I could even forget the moments that I smiled back at his impropriety or sat quietly as his hands roamed. It was easier to ignore my own failings when each new day brought a new narrative in which my own track record was immaterial.

Two things are important to understand about a narcissist's volatility and why it elicits not just our vigilance but our obsequiousness. In clinical terms, one is called "whole object relations," which concerns the narcissist's ability to understand themselves and others on both stable and nuanced terms as having both positive and negative qualities. Without whole object relations, there's no middle ground: people are either stellar or worthless, effective or pathetic, loyal or adversarial.[7] The second, called "object constancy," is the narcissist's capacity to maintain an emotional connection and positive feelings toward someone who has done something that upsets them or who is simply physically absent from their life.[8] When your boss lacks object constancy, there's no shared history to fall back on; your significance amounts to however they regard you in the moment. Taken together, these two deficits mean that to a narcissist you're either with them, you're against them, or you've entirely ceased to exist to them. And because those latter two spots are an untenable place to be professionally, more often than we'd like, we give them what they want.

A comedy writer in Los Angeles told me about coming to terms with how she indulged her former boss, whom she and multiple news reports described as both physically and psychologically abusive to his staff. She said that if her behavior toward him were examined in a courtroom, her character would be attacked based on the moments she flirted back, responded with a risqué joke, or sat on his lap. "I've had some time to process it and can now be nonjudgmental toward myself in terms of how I acted," she said. "I did whatever I could do to make things okay for myself. So, yeah, if I sat on his lap, I did it because it was going to buy me a moment of peace, because sacrificing my body usually quelled whatever narcissistic impulse he was acting out on. It was like putting a coin in a slot that would let things run safely for a couple of hours." Every bit we pay for momentary safety adds up, and soon we're giving of ourselves in ways that we never intended. The byproduct is our loyalty.

Anecdotally, many people had a need to justify the time they spent working for their narcissistic boss. Sometimes they emphasized an indisputable genius to his work. I noticed a trend in my conversations with Charlie's former staffers in which the longer they had worked for him, the more likely they seemed to believe in his unparalleled talent as an interviewer. Was it their own detached reverence for Charlie that had kept them at the show? Or was their reverence a coping mechanism—a kind of Stockholm syndrome in which they began identifying with their captor's own sense of grandiosity?

Still, for others, more often than not women, something that had complicated their boss's abuse, even long after they had left their jobs, was an insuppressible amount of compassion precisely *because* of his narcissism—the sense that his behavior was driven by unspeakable insecurity and torment and that, despite all his power, his life was pitiful, lonely, and devoid of meaningful relationships. Narcissism, after all, commonly stems from childhood abuse and neglect. And so, his cruelty notwithstanding, he received a steady flow of sympathy. I heard about their assumed impotence or possible closeted homosexuality and about the crippling insecurities they had with their height or weight. Even when allegations had already been levied and horrific behavior had been established, these women spoke off the record in an effort to spare their own abusers from any additional suffering.

We knew these men were not emotionally well, and indulging their self-narratives had at times felt merciful. A former journalist once found her narcissistic boss crying under his desk. He was too fat, he told her. She sat with him, comforting him with the assurances he needed to hear about his undeniable attractiveness. "I was always one of those people who drew on my own self-value as a fixer, somebody there to help you with your problems," she told me. "Maybe that's why he targeted me."

The Duke psychiatrist who oversaw the development of the fourth edition of the *DSM*, Dr. Allen Frances, asserts that the essential ingredient in any mental illness is suffering. In other words, does the person in question experience extreme distress and moments of debilitating despair?[9] For too many women, sparing their bosses from any such misery was a de facto part of their job. Many times it tapped their deep compulsion to tend to a man's ego—the traditional female role pressed upon women by the patriarchy that we witnessed with emotional labor.

One Saturday in April, I was working in the office when Charlie came in unexpectedly. He asked me what I was doing the next day, given that it was Easter, and suggested we do something. Maybe go to church? Out to eat? It was the first and only time there was no pretense of work in one of his invites. It would mean agreeing to hang out with him solely for the sake of hanging out. I was put on the spot—not to mention *completely* baffled by the suggestion of church. But I was also deeply unnerved by his loneliness and fragility in that moment. A man with no family and seemingly no meaningful friendships, roaming about the office until he saw me—a low-level producer in the wrong place at the wrong time. *Jesus Christ*, I thought as I agreed to an early Easter dinner.

My own tortured sympathy enabled both Charlie and his delusions. I was forced to think about this in 2017 when, in response to the accusations levied against him, he said something that other powerful men had implied in their own #MeToo defenses: "I always felt that I was pursuing shared feelings." The truth was that Charlie's narcissistic volatility had made it too terrifying to clarify to him otherwise. And why would I have risked it, or even bothered, when every day brought with it a new story?

"It's This Total Toxic Masculine Bullshit"

Recent history has shown us, quite unrelentingly, that the narratives of megalomaniacal men are difficult to rein in, their harm extending far beyond their immediate surroundings. Our public discourse, political norms, democratic system, pandemic responses, educational curriculums, X accounts, satellite networks—*nothing* is safe from the whims of their entitlement. And none of this would be the case if individually and collectively we weren't such suckers for male narcissists.

It's well established that narcissistic men have a penchant for sexual harassment and other forms of abusive behavior. But less recognized is our own penchant for narcissists—the fact that, in our culture, a personality short on empathy and high on self-importance is often construed as having the strength and tenacity that it takes to be a godsend. We know about power going *to* men's heads. When we invert this paradigm, however, and look at how an unearned sense of grandiosity can actually drive men's success, we're forced to reckon with the damage done by our specific perception of what constitutes leadership and male greatness. We might publicly bemoan whoever the high-profile narcissist du jour is, calling out their absurdity and detriment as such, but the formula behind their ascension remains uncontested. We fall for it, time and again.

Andrew Cuomo provides the perfect case study in how we conflate male narcissism with a kind of quintessential tough-guy flex that's necessary to get shit done. As New York governor, he was a ferocious bully and a consummate liar who never ceased changing his story in whatever way he could to protect his image as a strongman. In an extensive exposé on Cuomo's culture of misconduct and deception for *New York* magazine, Rebecca Traister uncovered how the governor's abject failures as a leader were obscured by his machismo and ruthlessness. "It's this total toxic masculine bullshit that disguises a very poorly run place," a former staffer told her.[10] In fact, it appeared to be run in whichever manner best served Cuomo's sense of superiority. When he wasn't verbally assaulting those who inconvenienced him, he was allegedly combing through event photos to identify attractive young women for his staff to track down and hire. When he wasn't scrubbing reports to downplay the number of Covid deaths in nursing homes statewide by as much as 50 percent, he was reportedly so neglectful of the state's census and subsequent redistricting that he can take some credit for costing Democrats the House of Representatives in the midterm elections following his resignation.[11]

Not long before leaving office in 2021, Cuomo was beloved by many who found solace in his no-nonsense schtick, which he projected in his daily, Emmy Award–winning press briefings to address the pandemic. Life in the time of Covid was unpredictable and scary, and with nothing more reassuring than a powerful, patriarchal archetype, Cuomo emerged as the straight shooter needed to save his people—the antidote to our nation's former reality TV star of a president who proudly pondered the medical efficacy of injecting household disinfectants into the human body. (Narcissism, after all, has no political affiliation.)

One evening after a Cuomo-themed Zoom happy hour with friends, New Yorker and self-proclaimed "Cuomosexual" Katie Nave sent the governor a message of gratitude for his leadership. Months later, after he finally resigned over sexual harassment allegations, Nave asked an important question in *Elle* magazine: "Why is it that our critical thinking skills so quickly fly out the window when a dominant, white man with an ego enters the arena?" She acknowledged that Cuomo's brutal scare tactics as a governor weren't exactly secret when she and so many others embraced him, fundamental flaws and all. "I have loved, worked for, and championed more toxic men in my life than I can even begin to count," she confessed. "From the press releases that I wrote for a nonprofit CEO—before he was eventually arrested for stealing from his own social services charity—to the abusive boyfriend that I defended tirelessly for years, I have laid down at the feet of these types of men far too many times."[12] Nave is *far* from alone.

Tomas Chamorro-Premuzic, professor of business psychology at University College London, studies the ways both individuals and organizations fall for the seduction of narcissistic leaders, whose air of supreme confidence draws us in and whose self-absorption, arrogance, and abrasiveness we misconstrue as male leadership. Such men are often incredibly charming masters of impression management and geniuses at selling their vision. They are very much in awe of themselves, especially in light of their actual talents.[13] And they are more often than not *really* crappy leaders.

As Chamorro-Premuzic explains, the very traits that we celebrate as signs of greatness are the same ones that predict these men's downfall.[14] Their self-absorption cripples their ability to manage collective efforts; they overpromise, underdeliver, and engage in antisocial behavior such as bullying, harassment, sexual misconduct, and sometimes even white-collar crime. Chamorro-Premuzic points out that when it comes to unethical behavior, it's not that all narcissists do these things. Rather, it's that when powerful and successful leaders do them, it's often *because* they're narcissists.[15] His broader concern, however, is that our very perception of leadership creates a systemic problem for women in which the innumerable career obstacles they face at work matter less to their professional trajectory than the *lack* of any such obstacles faced by their generally inept male peers. "The result," he writes, "is a pathological system that rewards men for their incompetence while punishing women for their competence."[16]

Such a "pathological system" was captured powerfully by Jennifer Barnett in her *Medium* essay titled "I Left My Career in Prestige Media Because of the Shitty Men in Charge and They Are Still in

Charge and Still Fucking Up." Barnett, a former managing editor of a highly respected magazine, maintains that a fair share of men at the publication were somehow untouchable no matter how lousy their judgment proved. Foremost among them was its editor in chief, also the president of America's principal organization for head editors of magazines and websites. And while she characterizes him as "shitty," a lot of the tendencies she describes about him could also be labeled "narcissistic." She reports that he had a remarkable sense of superiority and considered the work under his helm "beyond reproach." He had a rage problem that was directed largely at women, including his own assistant, to whom he had ceased to speak. He maintained in-groups and out-groups, with those in his favor constituting a select cadre of male editors who were free to walk into his office at any time to shoot the breeze. Toward those who weren't in his favor, he was astoundingly petty and vindictive. He would invite people into his office for a drink, making a display out of clinking glasses with everyone save for whom he held that day's grudge.

Barnett says she always had to adapt and maneuver behind the scenes to get work done without "tripping his rage wire." When things eventually reached a point where work was impossible to complete, she went to both HR and management, and was assured by higher-ups that something was being done. What they *did* was promote him to replace the magazine's president, who unexpectedly quit. The male narcissist who was making her job unbearable, and who still happened to be the president of her field's most important organization, emerged with even more power. And so, despite a career full of glowing performance reviews at one of the country's most prestigious magazines, she felt that she had no choice but to leave the industry.

Although she doesn't mention her boss by name, it's clear—or, at the very least, easily googleable—that Barnett is talking about the white, Ivy-educated editor in chief whom she worked under at the *Atlantic*. In 2017, while she was volunteering to write the newsletter for the parents' organization at her child's school, he was hired by the *New York Times* to be the editorial page editor— perhaps the most influential position in U.S. journalism. Soon after his arrival, he sought to expand the political perspectives his team published by enlisting a neoconservative male writer whose debut piece expressed skepticism of climate science, resulting in thousands of angry readers writing to the paper and a spike in canceled subscriptions. His tenure as editor lasted roughly four years, ending with his resignation over the decision to publish a GOP senator's call for the use of military force against Black Lives Matter protesters. From there he joined the *Economist*, where at the time of writing he is a visiting senior editor. "Why does it matter?" asks Barnett. "Because the same men who continually fuck up are still in charge of the media. They shape the world."[17]

Of course, one would be right to wonder if these men's professional resiliency was best described as the result of a pathological system or simply white male privilege. As one of Charlie's former female producers pushed back on the idea that he might be a narcissist, at least a clinical one: "If we can call it the mental disorder of being a white man, then, yeah, he had a disorder. His whole life he's been told that he can do whatever he wants."

Her observation echoes the work of Ijeoma Oluo, who eloquently argues that we have collectively conditioned white men to believe in their own automatic superiority. Her book *Mediocre: The Dangerous Legacy of White Male America* describes white male mediocrity as a "baseline," a "dominant narrative" that we work to preserve in our country regardless of white male skill or talent.

"When I talk about mediocrity," writes Oluo, "I am talking about how aggression equals leadership and arrogance equals strength . . . This is not a benign mediocrity; it is brutal. It is a mediocrity that maintains a violent, sexist, racist status quo that robs our most promising of true greatness."[18]

Whereas Chamorro-Premuzic's work uncovers our pathological system through extensive data collection, Oluo reveals it through our stories of white American manhood—the mythologies that have shaped our collective imaginations for the worse. Consider the nineteenth-century likes of William "Buffalo Bill" Cody, who—beyond his contributions to the genocide of Native Americans and the decimation of American buffalo—took largely embellished if not entirely fabricated stories of his own intrepidness on the road. The same kind of white male self-aggrandizement and disregard of inconvenient facts lives on in our politics, businesses, professional sports, and educational system.

For Oluo, while some have worked to preserve this system of mediocrity more than others, we have all played a part in a situation that benefits no one. "I do not believe that these white men are born wanting to dominate. I do not believe that they are born unable to feel empathy for people who are not them," she writes. "I believe that we are all perpetrators and victims of one of the most evil and insidious social constructs in Western history: white male supremacy."[19]

An Epidemic, Yours and Mine

"Every society reproduces its culture, its norms, its underlying assumptions, its modes of organizing experience—in the individual, in the form of personality," wrote historian Christopher Lasch in his landmark 1979 book *The Culture of Narcissism: American Life in an Age of Diminishing Expectations*. Lasch believed that radical economic and social change were resulting in the normalization of pathological narcissism. "Today men seek the kind of approval that applauds not their actions but their personal attributes . . . They want to be envied rather than respected. Pride and acquisitiveness, the sins of an ascendant capitalism, have given way to vanity," he lamented.[20]

Thirty years later, Jean M. Twenge and fellow academic psychologist W. Keith Campbell would provide data revealing that narcissism had since risen beyond Lasch's wildest imagination. In their book *The Narcissism Epidemic*, Twenge and Campbell informed us that narcissism had grown in tandem with American obesity. Whereas in the early 1950s, 12 percent of fourteen- to sixteen-year-olds agreed with the statement "I am an important person," by 1989 for that same age group, 77 percent of males and more than 80 percent of females agreed with the statement. In 1982, half as many college students answered the Narcissistic Personality Inventory in a narcissistic direction as compared to 2009. These indicators jibe with additional polling taken since the book's publication. In 2014, 59 percent of college freshmen rated their intellectual self-confidence above average—in 1966, it was 39 percent[21]—while a 2019 survey revealed that college students with narcissistic tendencies broadly embraced them as positive attributes.[22]

Twenge and Campbell's warning was about more than personality traits; it was about a change in cultural values with serious consequences, "including aggression, materialism, lack of caring for others, and shallow values."[23] Among the many culprits that they cited was our society's increased emphasis on individualism, the self-esteem movement of the 1980s, a change to a more indulgent parenting style, America's easy access to credit, and a surge in consumer culture and celebrity worship. "No single event initiated the narcissism epidemic," they write. "Instead, Americans' core cultural ideas slowly became more focused on self-admiration and self-expression. At the same time, Americans' faith in the power of collective action or the government was lost."[24]

A cultural shift in the prevalence of narcissism has very real implications for our enablement of abuse, be it systemic or capricious in nature. Studies show that narcissism is not only a predictor of sexism, with both narcissistic men and women more likely to hold sexist attitudes than their less narcissistic peers, it can also be a predictor of racist beliefs.[25] Becoming generally more narcissistic also means becoming generally less mindful of what others are experiencing and less invested in our collective well-being. It means becoming generally more inclined to disregard the discrepancy between one's ideal and one's real self. Essentially, becoming generally more narcissistic means becoming generally more complicit.

But let's go back to the sources cited by Twenge and Campbell for this state of affairs. While it may be that no one thing catapulted us along our path of self-absorption, there is one specific context with which the steep ascent of our narcissism trajectory chronologically aligns. You guessed it: neoliberalism. In fact, all the contributing factors cited by psychologists for increases in narcissism can be contextualized under its social and economic tenure.* Having chipped

---

* While former president Ronald Reagan carried the blazing torch of neoliberalism, its flame was kindled under his predecessor, Jimmy Carter, whose tenure accounts for the earliest dates in which social scientists began tracking our levels of narcissism. Carter, a peanut farmer who asked Americans to conserve energy and drive less, was also among a faction of Democrats who believed that the time had come to depart from New Deal principles and embrace free-market ones. During a time of enormous stagflation, he quietly slashed corporate taxes, deregulated the airlines and trucking industries, and began the deregulation of our telecommunications. "We really need to realize that there is a limit to the role and the function of government," he declared in his 1978 State of the Union address. "Bit by bit we are chopping down the thicket of unnecessary federal regulations by which government too often interferes in our personal lives and our personal business."

away at our well-being and sense of community while increasing our loneliness and sense of competition, neoliberalism pushed us further toward the pathological end of the narcissistic spectrum. It's continued to exacerbate the aggression, materialism, and lack of empathy about which Twenge and Campbell wrote fifteen years ago.

For those who remain suspect of the capacity for economic policy to impact personality, a compelling 2018 study took advantage of Germany's former East–West divide to find out if modern capitalistic cultures were better at nurturing narcissism. Researchers administered online tests to measure both narcissism and self-esteem among more than one thousand Germans, a portion of whom had grown up in the democratic, capitalist West, and a portion of whom had grown up in the communist East prior to the two countries' reunification in 1990. Even when controlling for age and gender, the results indicated that those who hailed from the West scored higher on narcissistic grandiosity. More compelling still was that participants from the East, despite their lower rates of narcissism relative to their western counterparts, scored higher in self-esteem. Researchers took care to distinguish the difference between the two attributes: "Narcissism and high self-esteem both include positive self-evaluations, but the entitlement, exploitation, sense of superiority, and negative evaluation of others that are associated with narcissism are not necessarily observed in individuals with high self-esteem."[26]

Paul Verhaeghe, professor of psychoanalysis at Ghent University in Belgium, has spent decades researching neoliberalism's impact on personality and argues that we're suffering the consequences of an economic system that *rewards* psychopathic tendencies. He writes: "Free-market forces and privatisation have taken their toll, as relentless pressure to achieve has become normative . . . I put this simple statement to you: meritocratic neoliberalism favors certain personality traits and penalises others."[27] Those traits, according to Verhaeghe, include a superficial articulateness that can win people over, along with an ability to showcase your talents, avoid responsibility for your behavior, and be an impulsive risk-taker. We do whatever it takes because neoliberalism makes success the criterion for a normal identity, and failure is the symptom of a disturbed one.

The Canadian author and physician Gabor Maté goes so far as to contextualize the effects of our current neoliberal culture in terms of trauma. In his book *The Myth of Normal: Trauma, Illness, and Healing in a Toxic Culture*, Maté details the health implications of an uptick in stress and inequality over recent decades to craft an indisputable picture of our own suffering—physically, emotionally, communally, spiritually. For Maté, we have lost compassion even for ourselves. "It is a marker of our culture's insanity that certain individuals who flee from shame into a shameless narcissism may even achieve great social, economic, and political success," he warns. "Our culture grinds many of the most traumatized into the mud but may also—depending on class background, economic resources, race, and other variables—raise a few to the highest positions of power."[28]

Such positions are frequently reached by means of the internet and social media, as with the former kickboxer and media personality Andrew Tate, who at the time of writing remains in Romania awaiting trial on charges of human trafficking. Tate is one of the world's most googled people, and his online videos mixing self-improvement and extreme misogyny have been viewed more than eleven billion times.[29] His appeal is so powerful among teenage boys that educators in the United Kingdom have begun mobilizing school forums to combat his broader message that women are the property of men to do with as they please. "He is brainwashing a generation of boys, and it's very frightening," a London teacher told the *New York Times*. "They seem to think he is right. He's right because he's rich."[30]

Tate is a prominent figure in today's "manosphere," a collection of online misogynistic communities that shares a heavy crossover with right-wing extremism.[31] Among this group are "incels," young men who describe themselves as "involuntarily celibate" and whose rage over this fact has resulted in dozens of murders and assaults over the past decade.[32] Most notorious was the 2014 Isla Vista killings carried out by Elliot Rodger, who on his "Day of Retribution" against women who had denied him sex and love, killed six people, women and men. We've entered a new age of entitlement far darker than anything documented by Twenge and Campbell.

Today, social psychologists warn that narcissism is threatening U.S. democracy, having studied the impact of what they say was Donald Trump's mobilization of a "national collective narcissism"— an in-group's belief that their greatness is insufficiently recognized. A 2021 study published in the *Analyses of Social Issues and Public Policy* showed that collective narcissism was more strongly associated with support for the disregard of democratic norms and the January 6 Capitol attack than any of the other variables considered, including education, racial resentment, and conservatism.[33] Also notable is that national collective narcissism produces in-group love and out-group hate; it predicts prejudice, retaliatory aggression, and a rejoicing in the suffering of others.[34]

However extreme we might consider these examples—however inapplicable they seem to our own lives—they're a part of the ecosystem in which we are all swimming. Our own habits and moral judgments become relative, our own ethical lapses easier to overlook, our own expectations excessive.

A common thread throughout so many stories of either sexual misconduct or other workplace abuse was a sense of indomitability that so often accompanies fame—even the slightest bit of it. In 2020, when the American chapter of the Court of Master Sommeliers was rocked by twenty-one women alleging either sexual harassment, manipulation, or assault by its male members, some were quick to lament the cultural ramifications the court had experienced with the success of the 2012 documentary *Somm*, after which candidate applications had increased by 20 percent.[35] The film featured the intensity and anxiety of candidates prepping for the final exam, along with the searing disappointment of those who failed and the blissful triumph of the select few who passed. Among the men featured—and *only* men were featured in the film—were established master sommeliers bestowing their expertise, some of whom would later be accused of sexual misconduct. Women had never had it easy in their elite, nearly all-white, nearly all-male club. But the celebrity experienced by some of the male sommeliers, along with the enthusiasm of others to be in its proximity, only ratcheted up the sense of male entitlement.

Richard Betts is a former master sommelier who, five months prior to the court's reckoning with sexual harassment, had resigned from the body over its inadequate, unsupportive response to the Black Lives Matter movement. Betts described to me the impact of *Somm* as having harmed the court's culture and integrity by attracting some who weren't interested in wine and service so much as they were fame and power. "It glorified this position, and then all of a sudden there's this new fetishization of the sommelier, and you have all these people wanting to get into the craft for the wrong reasons,"[36] he told me. "They want to be the cool guy. They want all this adoration. They want to be in the next movie—right? And then guess what? Some of these people pass. And *then* guess what? Some of those people get into positions of leadership."

The truth is that we don't have to be interested in fame to still be motivated by celebrity culture. The whole reason I stayed at *Charlie Rose* until I could get "producer" on my résumé was because his name carried sway. I knew it would open doors, and open they did. I never had a subsequent job interview in which the first question asked wasn't about Charlie and wasn't phrased with the sincerest of wonderment. My prior proximity to his brand of celebrity was more than a professional experience. It was respect and status.

When I was single and still lived in New York, Charlie's devoted following included men who expressed interest in me based on seemingly no other reason than that I had worked for him. After matching with a guy on the dating app Hinge, which allowed users to view the basic personal information listed on your Facebook profile, he initiated a direct message with the two-word question: "Charlie Rose?!" He was not the only man on the app to tell me that someday appearing on the show was one of his life's ambitions. One guy, unsolicited, messaged that if he could someday be inter-viewed by Charlie, he'd know that he'd reached a level of success as an entrepreneur with which he could be satisfied. These men annoyed me. Their fandom and desire for their own cause célèbre struck me as pathetic. Yet they were also the pudding in which I had strange proof that the emotionally scarring, horrific experience of having worked for a narcissist like Charlie had paid off—proof that I'd succeeded in taking a bit of cachet with me. And so, if they were pathetic, what was I?

The answer: a woman pursuing personal and professional ambi-tions of her own as best she knew how in a narcissistic culture.

Can We Imagine Differently?

In the years since the #MeToo movement began, I've worked hard at combating my own complicity, struggling to recognize all the ways that patriarchal narratives continue to shape my thinking. Humility is critical to this effort, and nothing has rubbed my face in the gap between my ideal self and the truth of my behavior quite like motherhood.

Like most parents, I'm selective about the media and entertainment to which my two young sons are exposed. I know how early unconscious gender biases begin cementing themselves. The diversity and messaging in the stories they read and watch have improved relative to my own childhood, and yet there's so much that remains problematic. Studies show, for example, that the percentage of female characters kids see on television in the United States and Canada has remained the same in recent decades, hovering steadily at about 30 percent. This is despite the growth in children's programming that features nonhuman characters, such as rescue dogs, pink pigs, robots, cars, airplanes, furry deep-sea explorers, and Lego action figures, for all of whom it's somehow still a man's world. As for the human characters, between 65 and 74 percent of them are white, with females more than twice as likely to be the token kid of color—or simply a racially ambiguous brunette with brown eyes.[1] When my children watch television (which is more often than I care to admit), I'll chime in when I think it's necessary to counter the narrative on the screen. "Is Miral scared of insects?" I ask my son about one of his female friends. Or: "The best skateboarder we know is Gemma, huh?"

But my intentions are often met by exhaustion and the deafening monotony of parenting's daily grind. In 2020, when my oldest son was five, we sat down together with a wordless picture book by the children's illustrator John Hare, *Field Trip to the Moon*. In it, a class of budding young explorers takes a yellow school bus–spaceship to the moon, where one of them is accidentally left behind. Yet he is not alone. Curious, gray, one-eyed Moonians emerge from the lunar sand to surround him, intrigued by his use of colorful crayons to pass the time. Follies ensue as the aliens delight in coloring upon themselves and their environment. When the school spaceship finally returns for the student, he boards it having kept his new friends a secret. This was the story as I had discussed it out loud with my son until we got to the last page, where the protagonist is seated safely without *her* space helmet—because the explorer is actually a girl, not a boy. I gasped in horror about my presumption. And while my son was quick to argue that it *could* be a boy, given that boys can have whatever hairstyle they want, my narrative default had already been exposed.

"He is the Subject; he is the Absolute," wrote Simone de Beauvoir. "She is the Other."

At bedtime more than a year later, I sat down with my younger son, age three, to look at Hare's second book, *Field Trip to the Ocean Deep*. A student is again left behind in the story, this time at the bottom of the ocean by a yellow submarine and while wearing a deep-sea helmet. Determined to redeem myself, I made sure that we discussed the lone child with the proper pronouns, not assuming they were either a boy or a girl, or gender binary for that matter. But again we got to the last page, and I was unprepared for the protagonist to be a *Black* boy. I didn't specifically think about the student being white, because I had the privilege not to; in my mind the student was raceless, which in our dominant culture *is* white. My default wasn't merely stories about male characters; it was stories about racially white ones.

I can cull Netflix all I want to make sure that my kids are watching programming with Black and brown people in it. I can carefully choose books that speak to inclusivity and gender equality because I know better than to instill in my children the notion that there is anything God-given or natural about a social hierarchy based on gender and race—especially when the vast majority of human history has, in fact, been spent living in egalitarian groups. And yet, at the literal end of my day, my imagination defaults to what is both male and white. I had failed in the most spectacularly fundamental way to transcend white patriarchy's hold on my own thinking—even as I was spending my days researching and writing a book about women's patriarchal conditioning.

Psychologists differentiate between two facets of the mind: one that is conscious, reflective, and intellectualizes, and one that operates outside our awareness, with an unwitting force fueled by our culture and the evolutionary expectations that were placed upon our ancestors. It's the latter that makes ending our complicity so challenging. Consider that the woman who coined the term "implicit bias"—the highly distinguished Harvard scientist whose research informed the world that ghostlike forces undermine our better, more moral, more consciously thinking selves—acknowledges that she herself exhibits sexist biases in her own assumptions. When Dr. Mahzarin Banaji takes what's known as the Implicit Association Test, her ability to associate scientific career words like "laboratory" or "biologist" with women does not come as automatically as her ability to associate such terms with men. "Utterly devastating" is how Banaji has described these results. "I ought to be able to associate male and female equally with science. I am, after all, a woman in science. To discover that I *cannot* do that, I think, is profound."[2]

Beyond relentless mindfulness, the task at hand is one of relentless imagination: Can we truly conceive of our lives outside of dominant, patriarchal frameworks? Can we conceive of a world not only in which power is shared equally by all women and men but where power manifests itself differently? And can we eat, sleep, and breathe that conception until it becomes a permanent fixture in our headspace?

This is a tall ask. But the truth is that we don't have an alternative. Gender inequality is the linchpin in an entire system of patriarchal norms and beliefs that have wrought and continue to exacerbate our most dire problems. We're at an unprecedented moment of historical change and, even if we wanted to, there's no going back to "normal." Climate change alone demands reimagining our lives and how we choose to conceive of our own well-being and abundance. Then throw in worsening global food crises, increasing human migration, the high likelihood of more pandemics, human genome editing, the undetermined impacts of automation and artificial intelligence, the reemergence of a nuclear threat, and the persistence of a deadly far-right extremism that debases truth and reality while vilifying science and expertise . . . We no longer have the luxury of indulging hyperindividualism or giving undeserved clout to the self-delusions of yet another male narcissist. Now is not the time to give deference where it's simply not due or fail to recognize intellect, talent, and ingenuity in whatever physical form or gender identity it comes packaged.

"It's the first time in history nobody has any idea how the world will look like in ten years," says the Israeli historian Yuval Harari.[3] This makes it a particularly opportune moment to create new stories. Building something better demands stories that recognize the reality of our lives as well as the truth of our potential—stories that are different from stories as we know them. Stories that don't reduce the hero's journey to individual feats of (male) greatness, but stories that celebrate inclusivity and collective welfare; that build community and trust; that decouple women's value and respect from the male gaze; that honor our individual agency without turning it into a liability; that recognize our physical and mental well-being as critical to achievement; that pay tribute to the count-less sources of personal meaning and happiness that have absolutely nothing to do with work or conspicuous consumption. Many such stories are out there, waiting to be told and heard on a loop. Other stories we'll need to create ourselves, and to do so with faith in one another, in our intentions and our capacity for change.

Okay, you might be thinking, *that sounds great in theory, but what does that mean in practice?* Millions of us saw exactly what it means when we went to see the blockbuster movie *Barbie* and witnessed the patriarchy's psychological hold over Barbieland vanish when America Ferrera's character Gloria began speaking to other women about the truth of their lived experiences. Stereotypical Barbie, played by Margot Robbie, put it perfectly: "By giving voice to the cognitive dissonance required to be a woman under the patriarchy you robbed it of its power!"

Let's take every opportunity we can to call out our patriarchal narratives and their harm. Let's do it at home, at work, and every-place in between. Let's be willing and candid enough to question our own behavior while practicing the change we'd like to see. And once we've started talking about things, we have to *keep* talking about them, because the traditional cultural narratives we're fighting have a powerful muscle memory. When people are exposed to counter-stereotypic notions involving gender, sexual orientation, and race, there is an immediate, beneficial effect—but one that tends to be short-lived because the exposure amounts to a one-off.[4] We must be relentless in our quest to give voice to the cognitive dissonance.

For all its genius, there's a critical flaw in filmmaker Greta Gerwig's *Barbie* that deserves our attention. Namely, matriarchal societies are not the inverse of patriarchal ones. The pioneering anthropologist Peggy Reeves Sanday, whose work addresses gender inequalities across cultures, asserts that Western notions about what a matriarchy is supposed to look like have it all wrong. After more than two decades studying the matriarchal Minangkabau people of West Sumatra, Indonesia, she contends that matriarchy is *not* about "female rule." When a society is profoundly shaped by a respect for the maternal and for nurturing, life is organized around principles of cooperation, not domination. Sanday recalls about her years living with the Minangkabau, "In answer to my persistent questions about 'who rules,' I was often told that I was asking the wrong question. Neither sex rules, it was explained to me, because males and females complement one another."[5] Similarly notable is that violence and sexual assault were highly unusual among the Minangkabau.[6] Sanday has also studied sexual coercion across 156 societies, and informs us that: "Men who are conditioned to respect the female virtues of growth and the sacredness of life do not violate women. It is significant that in societies where nature is held sacred, rape occurs only rarely."[7]

True change means venturing out of conventional comfort zones to conceive of the world differently. Many in the United States and other countries scoffed at Sweden's decision in the 2000s to drop personal pronouns in select public preschools as a part of its progressive gender-neutral pedagogy—when teachers began using the neutral pronoun *hen* in place of *han* (he) and *hon* (she). The change in language was part of a broader effort to safeguard students from being labeled while simultaneously encouraging them to explore the full range of their interests and emotions, which they did in classrooms where books, toys, and other learning resources were curated to avoid imparting traditional male-versus-female social expectations. Today, researchers report that these children are more open to new learning experiences and likely better equipped for future success. Studies also show that they're just as likely as their peers in traditional schools to categorize people by gender. The difference is simply that when they do, they're far less inclined to gender-stereotype, or to make implicit associations.[8] We can take inspiration from examples like this, which show not only the benefit of removing patriarchal imprints and other limits on our imaginations but the very possibility of doing so. And we can do the same with the accompanying imprints of white supremacy, neoliberalism, and hyperindividualism.

I'm confident, but maybe that's because I'm banking on our American optimism and belief in hard work. Maybe it's because I witnessed a movement like the one founded by Tarana Burke ignite the way it did: with enough women understanding the reality—the vast power differentials at play, the professional and legal risks, and the history of how women who have spoken out against harassment and sexual violence have been treated—and audaciously concluding, *Yeah, I'll do it. I'll tell the world about what happened to me.* I believe that we're more than equipped to consider this human experiment known as the patriarchy and similarly conclude, *Yeah, we can do differently.*

To begin to live our lives with a mindful intention that counters the narratives that have shaped our thinking—indeed, our very sense of self—is to dismantle the status quo from the inside out. I hold on tightly to the strange, holy-shit sensation that shook so many of us when the #MeToo reckoning first hit, when the world came into a different, sharper focus than what we had harmfully internalized. That sensation was our complicity being disrupted, and it's a power that lies within each of us—if we're willing to be open and honest enough to use it.

Acknowledgments

Little about the writing of this book went as planned, or at least not as scheduled. I am grateful for the patience and steadfast support of many.

I am *particularly* indebted to: Gillian MacKenzie, for representing me with tenacity as well as tender care; Rebecca Strobel, for being such an understanding editor extraordinaire; Karyn Marcus, for relentlessly championing this book's concept; Aimée Bell, for the confidence and the chance that came with it; and Sam Douglas, whose guidance and reassurance saved the day when all seemed hopeless. I am grateful to all those at Gallery Books who have lent their expertise and talent: Jennifer Bergstrom, Sally Marvin, Elisa Rivlin, Jen Long, Eliza Hanson, Caroline Pallotta, Nancy Tonik, Zoe Norvell, Lisa Litwack, Jill Siegel, and Bianca Ducasse.

My arguments relied on the research and reporting of too many to list, and whom I wish I could acknowledge with more than an endnote. These include journalists whose reporting led me to many of the women whose stories are in this book, as well as other inspiring, intimidatingly intelligent authors and academics, some of whom even graciously gave me their time when I know they had little to spare.

Before this journey, there was Matt Seaton, who took an essay I wrote about working for Charlie and made it stronger—strong enough, in fact, that it generated both the attention and inspiration for this book. Along the way, I made new friends who lent their publishing insights and other wisdom, including Jane Fransson and Hilary McClellan.

While writing this book, my anxiety and self-absorption were taken out on those I love most. I was not the mother, wife, daughter, sister, or friend I wanted to be. Thank you, Kerri, Missa, Leela, and Jenny for the check-ins. Thank you, Ana, Roxy, Tara, Molly, Tommy, Miranda, and Jeff for always being there. Thank you to Cheri and Duber for a lifetime of love and encouragement. Thank you, Sayer and Asa, for the affection and incessant comic relief. You get your kindness from your father, whose belief in this book meant as much to me as did his Instant Pot recipes and daily support. Thank you, Rich. I love you, the boys, and the crazy thing we've got going.

Notes

INTRODUCTION

1. Carol Gilligan and Naomi Snider, *Why Does Patriarchy Persist?* (Cambridge, UK: Polity Press, 2018), 8.

2. George E. Murphy, "Why Women Are Less Likely Than Men to Commit Suicide," *Comprehensive Psychiatry* 39, no. 4 (July–August 1998): 165–75, https://doi.org/10.1016/S0010-440X(98)90057-8; Stephanie Pappas, "APA Issues First-Ever Guidelines for Practice with Men and Boys," *Monitor on Psychology* 50, no. 1 (2019): 34, https://www.apa.org/monitor/2019/01/ce-corner.

3. bell hooks, interview by George Yancy, "bell hooks: Buddhism, the Beats and Loving Blackness," *New York Times*, December 10, 2015, https://archive.nytimes.com/opinionator.blogs.nytimes.com/author/bell-hooks/.

4. Barbara Bradley Hagerty, "An Epidemic of Disbelief," *Atlantic*, August 2019, https://www.theatlantic.com/press-releases/archive/2019/07/an-epidemic-of-disbelief-august-issue/594145/.

5. Advocates for Human Rights, "Sexual Harassment Is Conduct That Is Unwelcome or Unwanted," Stop Violence Against Women, February 2019, https://www.stopvaw.org/sexual_harassment_is_conduct_that_is_unwelcome_or_unwanted.

6. Larry Neumeister, Jennifer Peltz, and Michael R. Sisak, "Jury Finds Trump Liable for Sexual Abuse, Awards Accuser $5M," Associated Press, May 9, 2023, https://apnews.com/article/trump-rape-carroll-trail-fe68259a4b98bb3947d42af9ec83d7db.

7. Allison Archer and Cindy Kam, "Modern Sexism in Modern Times Public Opinion in the #Metoo Era," *Public Opinion Quarterly* 84, no. 4 (Winter 2020): 813–37, https://doi.org/10.1093/poq/nfaa058; Constance Grady, "The Mounting, Undeniable Me Too Backlash: How Susan Faludi's Feminist Classic Predicted This Moment," *Vox*, February 3, 2023, https://www.vox.com/culture/23581859/me-too-backlash-susan-faludi-weinstein-roe-dobbs-depp-heard.

8. Lisa Rabasca Roepe, "Why Workplace Harassment Increased During the Pandemic," *Fast Company*, July 19, 2021, https://www.fastcompany.com/90655155/why-workplace-harassment-increased-during-the-pandemic.

9. Kathryn Clancy, interview by Anna Casey, "Researcher: Sexual Harassment Just the 'Tip of the Iceberg,'" Illinois Public Media, April 25, 2019, https://will.illinois.edu/news/story/researcher-sexual-harassment-just-the-tip-of-the-iceberg.

10. Frank Dobbin and Alexandra Kalev, "Why Sexual Harassment Programs Backfire," *Harvard Business Review*, May–June 2020, https://hbr.org/2020/05/why-sexual-harassment-programs-backfire.

11. Author interview with Ana Gantman, assistant professor of psychology at Brooklyn College, March 10, 2022.

12. Jacob Engel, "Why Does Culture 'Eat Strategy for Breakfast'?," *Forbes*, November 20, 2018, https://www.forbes.com/sites/forbescoachescouncil/2018/11/20/why-does-culture-eat-strategy-for-breakfast/?sh=2725f0401e09.

13. Emma Brockes, "Sean Penn: 'Some of My Best Laughs Have Come Out of the Worst Reviews,'" *Guardian*, May 5, 2018, https://www.theguardian.com/film/2018/may/05/sean-penn-some-of-my-best-laughs-have-come-out-of-the-worst-reviews.

CHAPTER ONE: THE HIGH PRICE OF OUR FREE WILL

1. "Tony Robbins Rips Some Sex Abuse Victims for Trying to 'Make Themselves Significant,'" *CBS Mornings*, April 9, 2018, https://www.cbsnews.com/news/tony-robbins-asks-for-forgiveness-about-metoo-comments/; Butterscotch, "Tony Robbins and #MeToo—What Is Wrong with This Picture?," JN McC (Nanine McCool), March 26, 2018, accessed June 2023, YouTube video, 11:20, https://www.youtube.com/watch?v=74YILhy4RgE&t=188s (public access has since been discontinued).

2. "Tony Robbins' Apology on #MeToo Comments," Tony Robbins, https://www.tonyrobbins.com/tony-robbins-metoo-statement/#:~:text=Tony%20Robbins'%20Apology%20on%20%23MeToo%20Comments&text=I%20apologize%20for%20suggesting%20anything,a%20beautiful%20force%20for%20good.

3. "Leaked Records Reveal Tony Robbins Berated Abuse Victims," *BuzzFeed News*, May 18, 2019, YouTube video, 1:07, https://www.youtube.com/watch?v=G1ZT0YFMZN0.

4. "Leaked Records."

5. "Leaked Records."

6. Jane Bradley and Katie J. M. Baker, "Unlimited Power," *BuzzFeed News*, May 17, 2019, https://www.buzzfeednews.com/article/janebradley/tony-robbins-self-help-secrets.

7. Simon Carswell, "Self-Help Guru Tony Robbins Sues BuzzFeed in Irish Courts: Lawyer for US-Based Robbins Dismisses 'Libel Tourism' Claim over Defamation Action," *Irish Times*, November 27, 2019, https://www.irishtimes.com/news/crime-and-law/self-help-guru-tony-robbins-sues-buzzfeed-in-irish-courts-1.4097155; Shane Phelan, "US Self-Help Guru Tony Robbins Sues Twitter in Ireland," *Irish Independent*, April 17, 2020, https://www.independent.ie/irish-news/us-self-help-guru-tony-robbins-sues-twitter-in-ireland/39135836.html.

8. Bradley and Baker, "Unlimited Power."

9. The YouTube video made by the Date with Destiny attendee and "crazy bitch" Analay Souza Campos was eventually made private, but

was reported in news stories by Ephrat Livni, "Tony Robbins, the King of Self-Help, Finds Himself in Need of Assistance," *Quartz*, May 18, 2019, https://qz.com/1622776/tony-robbins-the-king-of-self-help-is-in-need-of-assistance; and Jackie Salo, "Tony Robbins Accused of Sexual Misconduct, Berating Rape Victims," *New York Post*, May 17, 2019, https://nypost.com/2019/05/17/tony-robbins-accused-of-sexual-misconduct-berating-rape-victims/.

10. Megan Twohey, "The Woman Defending Harvey Weinstein," February 7, 2020, in *The Daily*, produced by *New York Times*, podcast, 25:23, https://www.nytimes.com/2020/02/07/podcasts/the-daily/weinstein-trial.html.

11. Author interview with Kim Rubinstein, January 14, 2021.

12. Jonah Lehrer, "A Just World," *Atlantic*, September 1, 2009, https://www.theatlantic.com/daily-dish/archive/2009/09/a-just-world/196991/; Melvin J. Lerner and Carolyn H. Simmons, "Observer's Reaction to the 'Innocent Victim': Compassion or Rejection?," *Journal of Personality and Social Psychology* 4, no. 2 (1966): 203–10, http://web.mit.edu/curhan/www/docs/Articles/biases/4_J_Personality_Social_Psychology_203_(Lerner).pdf.

13. Lerner and Simmons, "Observer's Reaction."

14. Lehrer, "A Just World."

15. Author interview with Meredith Holley, January 21, 2021.

16. Author interview with Abby Schachner, January 20, 2021; Melena Ryzik, Cara Buckley, and Jodi Kantor, "Louis C.K. Is Accused by 5 Women of Sexual Misconduct," *New York Times*, November 9, 2017, https://www.nytimes.com/2017/11/09/arts/television/louis-ck-sexual-misconduct.html.

17. Richard Nisbett, "The Mistakes We All Make . . . and the Simple Experiment That Reveals It," *Guardian*, August 9, 2015, https://www.theguardian.com/science/2015/aug/09/world-in-context-mindware-tools-for-sharp-thinking.

18. Erica Goode, "How Culture Molds Habits of Thought," *New York Times*,

August 8, 2000, https://www.nytimes.com/2000/08/08/science/how
-culture-molds-habits-of-thought.html.

19. Goode, "How Culture Molds."

20. "Voters' Views Toward Justice Kavanaugh, #MeToo, and the Supreme
    Court: Results from a PerryUndem Survey of 1,000 Registered Vot-
    ers Using YouGov's Online Panel," PerryUndem Research/Communi-
    cation, September 27, 2019, https://view.publitas.com/perryundem
    -research-communication/perryundem-kavanaugh-and-metoo-report
    /page/1.

21. Robert Frank, *Under the Influence: Putting Peer Pressure to Work* (Prince-
    ton, NJ: Princeton University Press, 2020), 34.

22. Descriptions of the five #MeToo perpetrators listed in this paragraph, in
    order: Alexandra Berzon, Chris Kirkham, Elizabeth Bernstein, and Kate
    O'Keeffe, "Dozens of People Recount Pattern of Sexual Misconduct by
    Las Vegas Mogul Steve Wynn," *Wall Street Journal*, January 27, 2018,
    https://www.wsj.com/articles/dozens-of-people-recount-pattern-of
    -sexual-misconduct-by-las-vegas-mogul-steve-wynn-1516985953; Jane
    Mayer and Ronan Farrow, "Four Women Accuse New York's Attorney
    General of Physical Abuse," *New Yorker*, May 7, 2018, https://www
    .newyorker.com/news/news-desk/four-women-accuse-new-yorks
    -attorney-general-of-physical-abuse; Sonia Moghe, "Former New York
    AG Eric Schneiderman's Law License Has Been Suspended for a Year
    Over Allegations of Abuse," CNN Politics, April 28, 2021, edition.cnn
    .com/2021/04/28/politics/former-ny-ag-eric-schneiderman-law-license
    -suspended/index.html; Erik Wemple, "Opinion: Just How Did Matt
    Lauer's Famous Desk Button Work?," *Washington Post*, May 11, 2018,
    https://www.washingtonpost.com/blogs/erik-wemple/wp/2018/05/11
    /just-how-did-matt-lauers-famous-desk-button-work; Ashley South-
    all and Julia Moskin, "Police Close Sexual Assault Investigations of
    Mario Batali," *New York Times*, January 8, 2019, https://www.nytimes
    .com/2019/01/08/dining/mario-batali-sexual-assault-no-charges-nypd
    .html; Andrea Towers, "Elijah Wood Says an Orc in *Lord of the Rings*

Was Designed to Look Like Harvey Weinstein," *Entertainment Weekly*, October 5, 2021, https://ew.com/movies/elijah-wood-lord-of-the-rings -orc-harvey-weinstein-dax-shepard-podcast/.

23.   Catharine A. MacKinnon, preface to *Back Off! How to Confront and Stop Sexual Harassment and Harassers* by Martha Langelan (New York: Touchstone, 1993), 13–20; Ashleigh Spiliopoilou and Gemma L. Witcomb, "An Exploratory Investigation into Women's Experience of Sexual Harassment in the Workplace," *Violence Against Women* 29, no. 9 (July 2023): 1853–73, https://doi.org/10.1177/10778012221114921.

24.   Judd Apatow (@JuddApatow), X, November 9, 2017, 7:06 p.m., https://twitter.com/JuddApatow/status/928775787322281984.

25.   Jill Daly, "Words Matter: Computer Scientists Find Gender Bias as They Weigh #MeToo Media Coverage," *Pittsburgh Post-Gazette*, September 1, 2019, https://www.post-gazette.com/news/health/2019/09/01 Computational-gender-bias-MeToo-Carnegie-CMU-Ansari-media /stories/201908230135.

26.   Ajalie Field, Gayatri Bhat, and Yulia Tsvetkov, "Contextual Affective Analysis: A Case Study of People Portrayals in Online #MeToo Stories," paper presented at the Proceedings of the Thirteenth International AAAI Conference on Web and Social Media, Munich, June 2019, 158–69, https://ojs.aaai.org/index.php/ICWSM/article/view/3358/3226.

27.   Field, "Contextual Affective Analysis," 164.

28.   Virginia Alvino Young, "#MeToo Media Coverage Sympathetic to but Not Necessarily Empowering for Women," Carnegie Mellon University News, August 15, 2019, cmu.edu/news/stories/archives/2019/august /me-too-media-coverage.html.

29.   Peggy Cunningham, Minette E. Drumwright, and Kenneth William Foster, "Networks of Complicity: Social Networks and Sexual Harassment," *Equality, Diversity and Inclusion* 40, no. 4 (December 16, 2019): 392–409, https://doi.org/10.1108/EDI-04-2019-0117.

30.   Lisa Feldman Barrett and Eliza Bliss-Moreau, "She's Emotional. He's Having a Bad Day: Attributional Explanations for Emotion Stereotypes," *Emotion* 9, no. 5 (2009): 649–58, https://doi.org/10.1037/a0016821.

31. David Chang, interview by Michael Hainey, "David Chang: How to Create a Dining Empire," GQ, July 21, 2015, https://www.gq.com/video/watch /gq-a-david-chang-how-to-create-a-dining-empire.

32. Hannah Selinger, "Life Was Not a Peach," Eater, December 21, 2020, https://www.eater.com/22193151/momofuku-david-chang -memoir-eat-a-peach-review.

33. David Chang and Gabe Ulla, Eat a Peach: A Memoir (New York: Clarkson Potter, 2020), 164.

34. Chang's memoir and its "praise" can be found on his publisher's website: https://www.penguinrandomhouse.com/books/552829/eat-a-peach-by -david-chang-with-gabe-ulla/.

35. Bruckner's incident with Meier was first reported in Robin Pogrebin, "Women Say Richard Meier's Conduct Was Widely Known Yet Went Unchecked," New York Times, April 5, 2018, https://www.nytimes .com/2018/04/05/arts/design/richard-meier-sexual-misconduct-allega tions.html. Here, I am also relying on my own interview with Bruckner on January 17, 2021.

36. Richard Wike, "5 Ways Americans and Europeans Are Different," Pew Research Center, April 19, 2016, https://www.pewresearch.org /fact-tank/2016/04/19/5-ways-americans-and-europeans-are-different/.

37. Julia Isaacs, "International Comparisons of Economic Mobility," in Getting Ahead or Losing Ground: Economic Mobility in America, Brookings Institution, https://www.brookings.edu/wp-content/uploads/2016/07/02 _economic_mobility_sawhill_ch3.pdf.

38. Benjamin M. Friedman, "What's in a Name? Everything: Social Mobility Has Never Been Easy," Atlantic, July/August 2014, https://www .theatlantic.com/magazine/archive/2014/07/whats-in-a-name-every thing/372271/.

39. Dan McAdams, "American Identity: The Redemptive Self; 2007 Division One Award Addresses," General Psychologist 43 (Spring 2008): 20–27, https://www.sesp.northwestern.edu/docs/publications/20946 57112490a0f25ec2b9.pdf.

40. McAdams, "American Identity."

41. Bob Mondello, "Hollywood Dreams of Wealth, Youth, and Beauty," *All Things Considered*, NPR, June 19, 2012, https://www.npr.org/2012 /06/19/154861194/hollywood-dreams-of-wealth-youth-and-beauty.

42. L. J. Shrum, "Cultivation Theory: Effects and Underlying Processes," in *The International Encyclopedia of Media Effects* (New York: John Wiley & Sons, Inc., 2017), 1–12, https://www.researchgate.net/profile/L-Shrum/public ation/314395025_Cultivation_Theory_Effects_and_Underlying_Pro cesses/links/59dbad4d458515e9ab451b33/Cultivation-Theory-Effects -and-Underlying-Processes.pdf.

43. Shrum, "Cultivation Theory."

44. Gudbjörg Hildur Kolbeins, "The Non-Finding of the Cultivation Effect in Iceland," *Nordicom Review* 25, nos. 1–2 (August 2004): 309–14, https://doi.org/10.1515/nor-2017-0288. Here, Professor Kolbeins is paraphrasing Professor Mallory Wober, who, based on his own research, once said: "What may be true in America is not true in Britain."

45. George Gerbner, "Sex on Television and What Viewers Learn from It," Comments Prepared for the National Association of Television Program Executives Annual Conference, San Francisco, February 19, 1980, https://web.asc.upenn.edu/Gerbner/Asset.aspx?assetID=2480.

46. Richard Goldstein, interviewed by Knut Olav Åmås, "Culture and Gender in the Neoconservative USA," Samtiden/Eurozine, July 17, 2003, https:// www.eurozine.com/culture-and-gender-in-neo-conservative-america/.

47. Goldstein interview by Åmås, "Culture and Gender."

48. Steven Heine and Takeshi Hamamura, "In Search of East Asian Self-Enhancement," *Personality and Social Psychology Review* 11, no. 1 (2007): 4–27, https://doi.org/10.1177/1088868306294587.

49. Steve Loughnan et al., "Economic Inequality Is Linked to Biased Self-Perception," *Psychological Science* 22, no. 10 (October 2011): 1254–58, https://doi.org/10.1177/0956797611417003.

50. Facundo Alvaredo, Lucas Chancel, Thomas Piketty et al., "World Inequality Report 2018 Executive Summary," World Inequality Lab, 2018, https://wir2018.wid.world/files/download/wir2018-summary -english.pdf.

51. Heather Long, "U.S. Inequality Keeps Getting Uglier," *CNN Business*, December 22, 2016, https://money.cnn.com/2016/12/22/news/economy/us-inequality-worse/index.html.

52. Alexandre Tanzi and Mike Dorning, "Top 1% of U.S. Earners Now Hold More Wealth Than All of the Middle Class," *Bloomberg News*, October 8, 2021, https://www.bloomberg.com/news/articles/2021-10-08/top-1-earners-hold-more-wealth-than-the-u-s-middle-class.

53. Anthony Kammas, "What Is Neoliberalism? A Political Scientist Explains the Use and Evolution of the Term," USC Dornsife News, September 6, 2022, https://dornsife.usc.edu/news/stories/3755/what-is-neoliberalism.

54. George Monbiot, "Neoliberalism—the Ideology at the Root of All Our Problems," *Guardian*, April 15, 2016, https://www.theguardian.com/books/2016/apr/15/neoliberalism-ideology-problem-george-monbiot.

55. The assertion that the United States has been a capitalist country since its founding has been made by multiple historians, including Carl Degler and Jonathan Levy; Steven Hahn, "Land of Capital: The History of the United States as the History of Capitalism," *Nation*, November 1, 2021, https://www.thenation.com/article/society/jonathan-levy-ages-of-capitalism/.

56. Margaret Thatcher, interview by Ronald Butt, *Sunday Times*, as posted by Margaret Thatcher Foundation, May 3, 1981, https://www.margaretthatcher.org/document/104475.

57. Monbiot, "Neoliberalism."

58. Julia C. Becker, Lea Hartwich, and S. Alexander Haslam, "Neoliberalism Can Reduce Well-Being by Promoting a Sense of Social Disconnection, Competition, and Loneliness," *British Journal of Social Psychology* 60, no. 3 (July 2021): 947–65, https://bpspsychub.onlinelibrary.wiley.com/doi/epdf/10.1111/bjso.12438.

59. Guy Redden, "Is Reality TV Neoliberal?," *Television & New Media* 19, no. 5 (2018): 399–414, https://doi.org/10.1177/1527476417728377.

60. Yalda T. Uhls and Patricia M. Greenfield, "The Rise of Fame: An Historical Content Analysis," *Cyberpsychology Journal of Psychosocial Research on Cyberspace* 5, no. 1 (January 2011): article 1, https://cyberpsychology.eu/article/view/4243.

61. Jean Twenge, *Generations: The Real Differences Between Gen Z, Millennials, Gen X, Boomers, and Silents—and What They Mean for America's Future* (New York: Atria Books, 2023), 176–77.

62. Jonathan Donald Jenner, "Economic Crisis, Self-Blame, & the Dangerous Underbelly of the American Dream," Center for Popular Economics, November 4, 2015, https://www.populareconomics.org/economic -crisis-self-blame-the-dangerous-underbelly-of-the-american-dream/; Ofer Sharone, "Why Do Unemployed Americans Blame Themselves While Israelis Blame the System?," *Social Forces* 91, no. 4 (May 2, 2013): 1429–50, https://citeseerx.ist.psu.edu/viewdoc/download ?doi=10.1.1.887.7394&rep=rep1&type=pdf.

63. Maria Miceli and Cristiano Castelfranchi, "Reconsidering the Differences Between Shame and Guilt," *Europe's Journal of Psychology* 14, no. 3 (August 2018): 710–33, https://doi.org/10.5964/ejop.v14i3.1564.

CHAPTER TWO: THE HARM IN HARMONIZING

1. Jessica L. Lakin, Valerie E. Jefferis, Clara Michelle Chang et al., "The Chameleon Effect as Social Glue: Evidence for the Evolutionary Significance of Nonconscious Mimicry," *Journal of Nonverbal Behavior* 27 (2003): 145–62, https://doi.org/10.1023/A:1025389814290.

2. Bruce Hood, *The Self Illusion: Who Do You Think You Are?* (London: Constable, 2011), 138.

3. E. O. Wilson, "Biologist E. O. Wilson on Why Humans, Like Ants, Need a Tribe," *Newsweek*, April 2, 2012, https://www.newsweek.com /biologist-eo-wilson-why-humans-ants-need-tribe-64005.

4. Naomi Eisenberger and Matthew Lieberman, "Why It Hurts to Be Left Out: The Neurocognitive Overlap Between Physical and Social Pain," in *The Social Outcast: Ostracism, Social Exclusion, Rejection, and Bullying* (Sydney Symposium of Social Psychology, 2005): 109–27.

5. C. Nathan DeWall, Geoff MacDonald, Gregory D. Webster et al., "Acetaminophen Reduces Social Pain: Behavioral and Neural Evidence," *Association for Psychological Science* 21, no. 7 (2010): 931–37, https://doi .org/10.1177/0956797610374741.

6.   Gareth Cook, "Why We Are Wired to Connect: Scientist Matthew Lieberman Uncovers the Neuroscience of Human Connections—and the Broad Implications for How We Live Our Lives," *Scientific American*, October 22, 2013, https://www.scientificamerican.com/article /why-we-are-wired-to-connect/.

7.   Lakin et al., "The Chameleon Effect."

8.   Michael Bond, "We Get Infected by Other People's Emotions—and That's a Good Thing," *Discover*, March 25, 2015, https://www.discov ermagazine.com/health/we-get-infected-by-other-peoples-emotions -and-thats-a-good-thing.

9.   David Hamilton, *The Contagious Power of Thinking: How Your Thoughts Can Influence the World* (Carlsbad, CA: Hay House, 2011), 331; Evan Carr et al., "Differential States of Subjective Power Influence Spontaneous Facial Mimicry," Society for Neuroscience Meeting, New Orleans, October 15, 2012, https://www.sfn.org/~/media/SfN/Doc uments/Press%20Releases/2012/11Faces.ashx. Multiple studies have shown that women are more susceptible to emotional contagion, be it emotions of happiness or sadness, given their socialization to be nurturing and more responsive to the feelings of others. Among these studies is R. William Doherty, Lisa Orimoto, Theodore M. Singelis et al., "Emotional Contagion Gender and Occupational Differences," *Psychology of Women Quarterly* 19, no. 3 (1995): 355–71, https://doi .org/10.1111/j.1471-6402.1995.tb00080.x.

10. Janina Neufeld, Chun-Ting Hsu, and Bhismadev Chakrabarti, "Atypical Reward-Driven Modulation of Mimicry-Related Neural Activity in Autism," *Frontiers in Psychiatry* 10 (2019): 327, https://doi.org/10.3389 /fpsyt.2019.00327.

11. Esteban Ortiz-Ospina, "Who Do We Spend Time with Across Our Lifetime?," Our World in Data, December 11, 2020, https://ourworld indata.org/time-with-others-lifetime.

12. Association for Psychological Science, "Shared Pain Brings People Together, Study Concludes," *ScienceDaily*, September 9, 2014, www.sciencedaily .com/releases/2014/09/140909113340.htm.

13. Sebastian Junger, *Tribe: On Homecoming and Belonging* (New York: Twelve, 2016), 92.

14. *Chad Hudgens v. Prosper INC., and Joshua Christopherson: Brief of Appellant,* Utah Court of Appeals Briefs, Brigham Young University Law School, BYU Law Digital Commons, 2009, https://digitalcommons.law.byu.edu/cgi /viewcontent.cgi?article=2658&context=byu_ca3; Karl Vick, "Team-Building or Torture? Court Will Decide," *Washington Post*, April 13, 2008.

15. Stanley Milgram, *Obedience to Authority* (New York: Harper Perennial Modern Thought, 1974), 31.

16. Cari Romm, "Rethinking One of Psychology's Most Infamous Experiments," *Atlantic*, January 28, 2015, https://www.theatlantic.com/health /archive/2015/01/rethinking-one-of-psychologys-most-infamous-exper iments/384913/.

17. Rutger Bregman, *Humankind: A Hopeful History* (New York: Blooms-bury, 2020), 169.

18. Milgram, *Obedience to Authority*, 8.

19. Kitty Green, interview by Millicent Thomas, "What Can She Do? Kitty Green on the Assistant," *Girls on Tops*, May 1, 2020, https://girlsontopstees .com/blogs/read-me/what-can-she-do-kitty-green-on-the-assistant.

20. Margaret Heffernan, *Willful Blindness* (New York: Simon & Schuster, 2019), 150.

21. Heffernan, *Willful Blindness*, 153.

22. Margaret Heffernan, *Willful Blindness* (London: Simon & Schuster, 2019), 215.

23. United 4 Social Change, "The Smoky Room Experiment: Trust Your Instincts—Psychology Experiments Series," Academy 4 Social Change, February 28, 2021, YouTube video, 4:33, https://www.youtube.com /watch?v=LYENi9padNg&t=22s.

24. Arlie Russell Hochschild, *The Managed Heart* (Berkeley: University of California Press, 2012), 7.

25. Haley Swenson, "Please Stop Calling Everything That Frustrates You Emotional Labor," *Slate*, October 20, 2017, https://slate.com/human

-interest/2017/10/please-stop-calling-everything-that-frustrates-you
-emotional-labor-instead-ask-yourself-these-three-questions.html.

26. Author interview with Haley Swenson, September 22, 2021.

27. AG Letitia James, *Report of Investigation into Allegations of Sexual Harassment by Governor Andrew M. Cuomo*, State of New York Office of the Attorney General, Albany, NY, August 3, 2021, 47–48, https:// ag.ny.gov/sites/default/files/2021.08.03_nyag_-_investigative_report .pdf.

28. James, *Report of Investigation*, 47–48.

29. Charlotte Bennett, interview by Norah O'Donnell, "Exclusive: Former Cuomo Aide Details Governor's Alleged Sexual Harassment," *CBS Evening News with Norah O'Donnell*, https://www.cbsnews.com/video /extended-interview-with-cuomo-accuser-charlotte-bennett/.

30. "Exclusive: Former Cuomo Aide," *CBS Evening News*.

31. Terrence Real, interview by Don Hazen and Kali Holloway, "Patriarchy and Toxic Masculinity Are Dominating America Under Trump," *Salon*, August 1, 2017, https://www.salon.com/2017/08/01/patriarchy -and-toxic-masculinity-are-dominating-america-under-trump_partner/.

32. Caprino, "Gender, Power and Relationships."

33. Author interview with Kyle Godfrey-Ryan, June 14, 2020.

CHAPTER THREE: THE MYTH OF WHO WE THINK WE ARE

1. Bruce Hood, *The Self Illusion: Who Do You Think You Are?* (London: Constable, 2011), 114.

2. Elizabeth Lesser, *Cassandra Speaks: When Women Are the Storytellers, the Human Story Changes* (New York: Harper Wave, 2020), 20.

3. Liz Meriwether, "I'm a Coward," *The Cut*, October 10, 2017, https://www .thecut.com/2017/10/im-a-coward.html.

4. Will Storr, *Selfie: How the West Became Self-Obsessed* (London: Picador, 2017), 66.

5. Charlize Theron, interview by Terry Gross, "Charlize Theron Reflects on Growing Up in South Africa During the Apartheid Era," *Fresh Air*,

NPR, July 17, 2020, https://www.npr.org/2020/07/17/891848562 /charlize-theron-reflects-on-growing-up-in-south-africa-during-the-apart heid-era#:~:text=And%20so%20my%20impression%20of,know%20 where%20that%20came%20from.

6. Michael S. Gazzaniga, *Who's in Charge? Free Will and the Science of the Brain* (New York: HarperCollins, 2011).

7. Hood, *The Self Illusion*, 170.

8. Michael Gazzaniga, "The Storyteller in Your Head," *Discover*, March 1, 2012, https://www.discovermagazine.com/mind/the-storyteller-in-your-head.

9. Ana P. Gantman, Marieke A. Adriaanse, Peter M. Gollwitzer et al., "Why Did I Do That? Explaining Actions Activated Outside of Awareness," *Psychonomic Bulletin & Review* 24 (2017): 1563–72, https://doi .org/10.3758/s13423-017-1260-5.

10. Jen Percy, "What People Misunderstand About Rape," *New York Times*, August 22, 2023, https://www.nytimes.com/2023/08/22/magazine /immobility-rape-trauma-freeze.html.

11. The work of psychologists Carol Gilligan and Naomi Snider posits that the patriarchy demands women be selfless and have relationships that serve men's needs (Carol Gilligan and Naomi Snider, *Why Does Patriarchy Persist?* [Cambridge: Polity Press, 2018], 6). As also noted on the topic of emotional labor in Chapter Two, author and family therapist Terrence Real believes that one of the unrecognized psychological compulsions at play in personal relationships is a feminine impulse to protect the male sense of self. It's an inclination familiar to many who have written about the topic of sexual harassment and assault, including the journalist Zosia Bielski, who, in reporting on the trial concerning CBC host Jian Ghomeshi's assault allegations, labeled it "politeness conditioning" (Zosia Bielski, "How Politeness Conditioning Can Lead to Confusion About Sexual Assaults," *Globe and Mail*, March 20, 2016, https://www.theglobeandmail.com/life/relationships/how -politeness-conditioning-can-lead-to-confusion-about-sexual-assults /article29294471/).

12. Cynthia Griffin Wolff, "A Mirror for Men: Stereotypes of Women in Literature," *Massachusetts Review* 13, no.1/2 (Winter–Spring 1972): 205–18, http://www.jstor.org/stable/25088222.

13. Hannah Thomas-Peter, "Exclusive: Video Shows Harvey Weinstein Behaving Inappropriately," *Sky News*, September 13, 2018, YouTube video, 8:36, https://www.youtube.com/watch?v=hC4eog5cY9Q.

14. David Friend, *The Naughty Nineties* (New York: Twelve, 2017), 4.

15. Author interview with Filipa Melo Lopes, April 22, 2022.

16. Tracy Clark-Flory, *Want Me: A Sex Writer's Journey into the Heart of Desire* (New York: Penguin Books, 2021), 30–31.

17. Mary Pipher, *Reviving Ophelia: Saving the Selves of Adolescent Girls* (New York: Penguin Group, 1994), 12.

18. Pipher, *Reviving Ophelia*, 35–36.

19. Mary Pipher and Sara Pipher Gilliam, interview by Rachel Martin, *All Things Considered*, NPR, June 30, 2019, https://www.npr.org/2019/06/30/737478316/reviving-ophelia-turns-25.

20. Twenge, *Generations*, 157.

21. That U.S. adolescents watched more television in the 1990s than they do today is documented in J. M. Twenge, G. N. Martin, and G. H. Spitzberg, "Trends in U.S. Adolescents' Media Use, 1976–2016: The Rise of Digital Media, the Decline of TV, and the (Near) Demise of Print," *Psychology of Popular Media Culture* 8, no. 4 (2019): 329–45, https://doi.org/10.1037/ppm0000203.

22. Jocelyn Noveck, "Pop Culture in the 2010s Put a Spotlight on Diversity and Inclusion," *PBS News Hour*, December 26, 2019, https://www.pbs.org/newshour/arts/pop-culture-in-the-2010s-put-a-spotlight-on-diversity-and-inclusion.

23. Allison Yarrow, *90s Bitch: Media, Culture, and the Failed Promise of Gender Equality* (New York: Harper Perennial, 2018), xvii.

24. Yarrow, *90s Bitch*, xvi–xvii.

25. Juliet Kahn, "SNL Sketches That Went Too Far," *Looper*, December 29, 2020, https://www.looper.com/170057/snl-sketches-that-went-too

-far/; Susan Baer, "Satirists Avoid Chelsea-Bashing," *South Florida Sun Sentinel*, July 25, 1993.

26. Shelly Grabe and Janet Shibley Hyde, "Body Objectification, MTV, and Psychological Outcomes Among Female Adolescents," *Journal of Applied Social Psychology* 39, no. 12 (2009): 2840–58, https://doi .org/10.1111/j.1559-1816.2009.00552.x.

27. Ariel Levy, *Female Chauvinist Pigs: Women and the Rise of Raunch Culture* (New York: Free Press, 2005), 4.

28. Levy, *Female Chauvinist Pigs*, 33.

CHAPTER FOUR: CONSENT CONTEXTUALIZED

1. Author interview with Marie-Louise Friedland, January 20, 2021.

2. Moira Donegan, "How #MeToo Revealed the Central Rift within Feminism Today," *Guardian*, May 11, 2018, https://www.theguardian.com /news/2018/may/11/how-metoo-revealed-the-central-rift-within-femi nism-social-individualist.

3. Ramin Setoodeh, "Inside Matt Lauer's Secret Relationship with a 'Today' Production Assistant," *Variety*, December 14, 2017, https://variety .com/2017/tv/news/matt-lauer-today-secret-relationship-production -assistant-1202641040/.

4. Setoodeh, "Inside Matt Lauer's Secret Relationship."

5. Setoodeh, "Inside Matt Lauer's Secret Relationship."

6. Dianna Pierce Burgess, "Guest Addie Collins Zinone: The Anatomy of Courage," *Press Forward Podcast*, October 2019, episode 3, part 1, 29:26, https://open.spotify.com/episode/6ZpuleqEFxCZRff3EDaoYp.

7. Burgess, "Guest Addie Collins Zinone," 29:26, https://open.spotify.com /episode/6ZpuleqEFxCZRff3EDaoYp; and Burgess, "Guest Addie Collins Zinone," October 2019, episode 3, part 2, 46:27, https://open.spotify.com /episode/4fJy71G9ZZ0TJSpBAgbP3T.

8. Paul Farhi, "'I Don't Want to Sit on Your Lap,' She Thought. But, She Alleges, Mark Halperin Insisted," *Washington Post*, October 26, 2017, https://www.washingtonpost.com/lifestyle/style/i-dont-want-to-sit-on

-your-lap-she-said-but-mark-halperin-insisted/2017/10/26/0baa883c
-ba64-11e7-9e58-e6288544af98_story.html.

9. Jim Hopper, "How Reliable Are the Memories of Sexual Assault Victims? The Expert Testimony Excluded from the Kavanaugh Hearing," *Scientific American*, September 27, 2018, https://blogs.scientificamerican.com/observations/how-reliable-are-the-memories-of-sexual-assault-victims/.

10. M. J. Layman, C. A. Gidycz, and S. J. Lynn, "Unacknowledged Versus Acknowledged Rape Victims: Situational Factors and Posttraumatic Stress," *Journal of Abnormal Psychology* 105, no. 1 (1996):124–31, https://doi.org/10.1037/0021-843X.105.1.124.

11. Laura C. Wilson and Katherine E. Miller, "Meta-Analysis of the Prevalence of Unacknowledged Rape," *Trauma, Violence, & Abuse* 17, no. 2 (2016): 149–59, https://doi.org/10.1177/1524838015576391.

12. Heather Murphy, "What Experts Know About Men Who Rape," *New York Times*, October 30, 2017, https://www.nytimes.com/2017/10/30/health/men-rape-sexual-assault.html.

13. Jessica Knoll, "I Dated My Rapist," *The Cut*, October 17, 2017, https://www.thecut.com/2017/10/i-dated-my-rapist-jessica-knoll.html.

14. Knoll, "I Dated My Rapist."

15. Caitlin Flanagan, "The Humiliation of Aziz Ansari," *Atlantic*, January 14, 2018, https://www.theatlantic.com/entertainment/archive/2018/01/the-humiliation-of-aziz-ansari/550541/.

16. Ashleigh Banfield, "Banfield Slams Ansari Accuser in Open Letter," CNN, January 16, 2018, YouTube video, 4:25, https://www.youtube.com/watch?v=y4bAULTwAJU.

17. Condoleezza Rice, "Condoleezza Rice on #MeToo: Let's Not Turn Women into Snowflakes," CNN, January 14, 2018, YouTube video, 2:53, https://www.youtube.com/watch?v=I8eToRjhAb0.

18. Stassa Edwards, "The Backlash to #MeToo Is Second-Wave Feminism," *Jezebel*, January 11, 2018, https://jezebel.com/the-backlash-to-metoo-is-second-wave-feminism-1821946939.

19. Anna North, "The #MeToo Generation Gap Is a Myth," *Vox*, March 20, 2018, https://www.vox.com/2018/3/20/17115620/me-too-sexual-harassment-sex-abuse-poll; Yuki Noguchi, "Are There Generational Differences When It Comes to Sexual Harassment at Work?," *All Things Considered*, NPR, December 12, 2017, https://www.npr.org/2017/12/12/569181017/are-there-generational-differences-when-it-comes-to-sexual-harassment-at-work.

20. Bobby Duffy, *The Generation Myth: Why When You're Born Matters Less Than You Think* (New York: Basic Books, 2021), 1.

21. As done by CBS News in 2019 (Jean Twenge, *Generations: The Real Differences Between Gen Z, Millennials, Gen X, Boomers, and Silents—and What They Mean for America's Future* [New York: Atria Books, 2023], 151).

22. Richard Fry, "Millennials Overtake Baby Boomers as America's Largest Generation," Pew Research Center, April 28, 2020, https://www.pewresearch.org/short-reads/2020/04/28/millennials-overtake-baby-boomers-as-americas-largest-generation/.

23. Paul Taylor and George Gao, "Generation X: America's Neglected 'Middle Child,'" Pew Research Center, June 5, 2014, https://www.pewresearch.org/short-reads/2014/06/05/generation-x-americas-neglected-middle-child/.

24. Lynn Phillips, *Flirting with Danger: Young Women's Reflections on Sexuality and Domination* (New York: New York University Press, 2000), 10.

25. Phillips, *Flirting with Danger*, 103.

26. Phillips, 96.

27. Phillips, 7.

28. Laina Y. Bay-Cheng, "The Agency Line: A Neoliberal Metric for Appraising Young Women's Sexuality," *Sex Roles* 73 (2015): 279–91, https://doi.org/10.1007/s11199-015-0452-6.

29. Bay-Cheng, "The Agency Line," 279–91.

CHAPTER FIVE: FOOT SOLDIERING IN STILETTOS

1. Jana Byars, "We Are Not Born Submissive: How Patriarchy Shapes Women's Lives," July 9, 2021, in *Ideas Podcast*, produced by Princeton University

Press, podcast, 11:03, https://press.princeton.edu/ideas/ideas-podcast-we
-are-not-born-submissive.

2. Cady Lang, "How the 'Karen Meme' Confronts the Violent History of White Womanhood," *Time*, https://time.com/5857023/karen -meme-history-meaning/.

3. Jessie Daniels, *Nice White Ladies: The Truth About White Supremacy, Our Role in It, and How We Can Help Dismantle It* (New York: Seal Press, 2021), 7.

4. Tressie McMillan Cottom, *Thick: And Other Essays* (New York: The New Press, 2019), 52.

5. Tressie McMillan Cottom, "Brown Body, White Wonderland," *Slate*, August 29, 2013, https://slate.com/human-interest/2013/08/miley -cyrus-vma-performance-white-appropriation-of-black-bodies.html.

6. McMillan Cottom, *Thick*, 60.

7. Lottie Joiner, "How Discrimination in the Workplace Impacts Black Women's Health and Well-Being," *Success*, May 30, 2023, https://www.success .com/how-discrimination-in-the-workplace-impacts-black-womens -health-well-being/; Kat Stafford, "Why Do So Many Black Women Die in Pregnancy? One Reason: Doctors Don't Take Them Seriously," Associated Press, May 23, 2023, https://projects.apnews.com/features/2023 /from-birth-to-death/black-women-maternal-mortality-rate.html; Jameta Nicole Barlow, "Black Women, the Forgotten Survivors of Sexual Assault," American Psychological Association, February 1, 2020, https://www .apa.org/topics/sexual-assault-harassment/black-women-sexual-violence.

8. Barlow, "Black Women, the Forgotten Survivors."

9. Verónica Caridad Rabelo, Kathrina J. Robotham, and Courtney L. McCluney, "'Against a Sharp White Background': How Black Women Experience the White Gaze at Work," *Gender, Work & Organization* 28, no. 5 (September 2021): 1840–58, https://doi.org/10.1111 /gwao.12564.

10. Rebecca Carroll, *Surviving the White Gaze: A Memoir* (New York: Simon & Schuster, 2021), 291–92.

11. Rebecca Carroll, "My Experience at Charlie Rose Went Beyond Sexism,"

Esquire, December 2, 2017, https://www.esquire.com/entertainment/tv/a13978884/charlie-rose-sexual-harassment-accuser-story/.

12. Polly Young-Eisendrath, *Women and Desire: Beyond Wanting to Be Wanted* (New York: Three Rivers Press, 2000), 3–4.

13. Jessa Crispin, *Why I Am Not a Feminist: A Feminist Manifesto* (Brooklyn: Melville House, 2017), 120.

14. Mahzarin Banaji and Anthony Greenwald, *Blind Spot* (New York: Bantam Books, 2016), 116.

15. *Women in the Workplace 2022*, McKinsey & Company, n.d., https://www.mckinsey.com/~/media/mckinsey/featured%20insights/diversity%20and%20inclusion/women%20in%20the%20workplace%202022/women-in-the-workplace-2022.pdf.

16. Alexandra Berkowitz and Irene Padavic, "Getting a Man or Getting Ahead," *Journal of Contemporary Ethnography* 27, no. 4 (January 1999): 530–57, https://doi.org/10.1177/089124199129023325.

17. Nyasha Junior, "Stop Calling Black Women 'Superheroes,'" *Dame*, July 12, 2018, https://www.damemagazine.com/2018/07/12/stop-calling-black-women-superheroes/.

18. Dianna Mazzone, "The Average Woman Spends HOW Much Time Getting Beautified?," *Refinery29*, February 28, 2014, https://www.refinery29.com/en-us/2014/02/63501/women-beauty-routines-time-survey; Sissi Johnson, "How Much Is Your Face Worth? American Women Average $8 per Day," *HuffPost*, March 8, 2017, https://www.huffpost.com/entry/how-much-is-your-face-worth-american-women-average_b_58befa65e4b06660f479e594.

19. Angela McRobbie, interview by Nigel Warburton, *Angela McRobbie on the Illusion of Equality for Women*, Social Science Space, June 3, 2013, https://www.socialsciencespace.com/2013/06/angela-mcrobbie-on-the-illusion-of-equality-for-women/.

20. Andi Zeisler, *We Were Feminists Once: From Riot Grrrl to Covergirl®, the Buying and Selling of a Political Movement* (New York: PublicAffairs, 2016), 20.

21. Ross Pomeroy, "Orgasm Gap: The Insidious Reason Women Have Fewer Orgasms Than Men," Big Think, May 13, 2022, https://bigthink.com /health/orgasm-gap-women-men/.

22. Ada Calhoun, *Why We Can't Sleep: Women's New Midlife Crisis* (New York: Grove Press, 2020), 7.

23. Robin R. Means Coleman and Emily C. Yochim, "Symbolic Annihilation," *The International Encyclopedia of Communication*, June 5, 2008, https://doi.org/10.1002/9781405186407.wbiecs124.

24. Carina Chocano, interview by Elizabeth Kiefer, "Are You the Cool Girl or the Princess? Neither—& That's the Problem," *Refinery29*, August 7, 2017, https://www.refinery29.com/en-us/2017/08/166365/carina -chocano-you-play-the-girl-interview.

CHAPTER SIX: SHOW NO WEAKNESS

1. David Graham-Caso (@dgrahamcaso), X, April 7, 2021, 8:33 a.m., https://twitter.com/dgrahamcaso/status/1380000781856768000; Tatiana Siegel, "'Everyone Just Knows He's an Absolute Monster': Scott Rudin's Ex-Staffers Speak Out on Abusive Behavior," *Hollywood Reporter*, April 7, 2021, https://www.hollywoodreporter.com/movies /movie-news/everyone-just-knows-hes-an-absolute-monster-scott -rudins-ex-staffers-speak-out-on-abusive-behavior-4161883/; Anne Victoria Clark, Jackson McHenry, Lila Shapiro et al., "Scott Rudin, As Told by His Assistants: A Portrait of a Toxic Workplace," *Vulture*, April 22, 2021, https://www.vulture.com/2021/04/scott-rudin-as -told-by-his-assistants.html.

2. David Graham-Caso (@dgrahamcaso), X, April 7, 2021, 11:33 p.m., https://twitter.com/dgrahamcaso/status/1380000781856768000; Gene Maddaus, "Friends of Scott Rudin's Late Assistant Speak Out on Producer's Abuses: 'He Was So Terrified of That Man,'" *Variety*, April 19, 2021, https://variety.com/2021/film/news/scott-rudin-kevin -graham-caso-assistant-1234954914/.

3. Clark et al., "Scott Rudin."

4. Sarah Stewart Holland and Beth Silvers, "The Glamorization of Work," May 9, 2018, in *The Nuanced Life*, podcast, 46:16, https://www.scribd.com/listen/podcast/419013410.

5. Silvia Bellezza, Neeru Baharia, and Anat Keinan, "Conspicuous Consumption of Time: When Busyness and Lack of Leisure Time Become a Status Symbol," *Journal of Consumer Research* 44, no. 1 (June 2017): 118–38, https://doi.org/10.1093/jcr/ucw076.

6. Erin Griffith, "Why Are Young People Pretending to Love Work?," *New York Times*, January 26, 2019, https://www.nytimes.com/2019/01/26/business/against-hustle-culture-rise-and-grind-tgim.html.

7. Elon Musk (@elonmusk), X, November 26, 2018, 4:49 p.m., https://twitter.com/elonmusk/status/1067173497909141504.

8. Benjamin Hunnicutt, "Work Is Our Religion and It's Failing Us," *HuffPost*, May 18, 2018, https://www.huffpost.com/entry/post-work-world_n_5afbe686e4b0779345d43a20.

9. Charles Ward, "Protestant Work Ethic That Took Root in Faith Is Now Ingrained in Our Culture," *Houston Chronicle*, September 1, 2007, https://www.chron.com/life/houston-belief/article/Protestant-work-ethic-that-took-root-in-faith-is-1834963.php.

10. Dina Vaccari, "I Was Quoted in the *NY Times* Article About Working at Amazon. Here Is *My* Story," *Medium*, August 31, 2015, https://medium.com/@dinavaccari/i-was-quoted-in-the-ny-times-article-about-working-at-amazon-4fd2667b2e35.

11. Glenn Collins, "The Psychology of the Cult Experience," *New York Times*, March 15, 1982.

12. Heffernan, *Willful Blindness*, 158.

13. *Working Conditions Survey*, Goldman Sachs Investment Banking Division, February 2021, https://drive.google.com/file/d/1jyeu-wvS3Z10xQ0BlMIDOkh_INoP_Nnb/view.

14. Jen Wieczner, "Revolt of the Goldman Juniors: Crushed by Pandemic Workloads, Wall Street's Youngest Want More Money and Better Conditions. But Mostly More Money," Intelligencer, *New York* magazine, November 4, 2021, https://nymag.com/intelligencer/2021/11

/goldman-sachs-analysts-money-pandemic.html?campaign_id=4&em
c=edit_dk_20211105&instance_id=44680&nl=dealbook.

15. Jennifer L. Berdahl, Marianne Cooper, Peter Glick et al., "Work as a Masculinity Contest," *Journal of Social Issues* 74, no. 3 (September 2018): 422–48, https://doi.org/10.1111/josi.12289.

16. Jennifer Berdahl, Peter Glick, and Marianne Cooper, "How Masculinity Contests Undermine Organizations, and What to Do About It," *Harvard Business Review*, November 2, 2018, https://hbr.org/2018/11/how-mas culinity-contests-undermine-organizations-and-what-to-do-about-it.

17. Nancy Beauregard, Alain Marchand, Jaunathan Bilodeau et al., "Gendered Pathways to Burnout: Results from the SALVEO Study," *Annals of Work Exposures and Health* 62, no. 4 (May 2018): 426–37, https://doi .org/10.1093/annweh/wxx114.

18. Gill Malinsky, "'Work Is the Single Most Important Way of Proving Your Worth' in the U.S., Says Professor—Why It's Making Us Miserable," CNBC Make It, March 2, 2021, https://www.cnbc .com/2021/03/02/why-americas-obsession-with-work-is-making -us-miserable-psychology-professors.html.

19. Derek Thompson, "America's Fever of Workaholism Is Finally Breaking," *Atlantic*, January 31, 2023, https://www.theatlantic.com/newsletters /archive/2023/01/american-rich-men-work-less-hours-workism /672895/; Derek Thompson, "Workism Is Making Americans Miserable," *Atlantic*, February 24, 2019, https://www.theatlantic.com /ideas/archive/2019/02/religion-workism-making-americans-miserable /583441/.

20. Juliana Menasche Horowitz and Nikki Graf, "Most U.S. Teens See Anxiety and Depression as a Major Problem Among Their Peers," Pew Research Center, February 20, 2019, https://www.pewresearch.org /social-trends/2019/02/20/most-u-s-teens-see-anxiety-and-depression -as-a-major-problem-among-their-peers/.

21. Elizabeth Kamarck Minnich, *The Evil of Banality: On the Life and Death Importance of Thinking* (Lanham, MD: Rowman & Littlefield, 2016), 169–70.

22. "Love Your Job? Someone May Be Taking Advantage of You," Duke
     Fuqua School of Business, April 24, 2019, https://www.fuqua.duke
     .edu/duke-fuqua-insights/kay-passion-exploitation.

23. Terry Nguyen, "Gen Z Does Not Dream of Labor," *Vox*, April 22, 2022,
     https://www.vox.com/the-highlight/22977663/gen-z-antiwork-capi
     talism.

24. Kathi Weeks, interview by Alyson Cole and Robyn Marasco, "Ask a
     Political Scientist: A Conversation with Kathi Weeks About the Politics
     of Work and the Work of Political Theory," *Polity* 53, no. 4 (October
     2021): 743–52, https://doi.org/10.1086/716085.

25. Author interview with Melanie Nichol, April 16, 2021.

26. Alex Steed and Sarah Marshall, "*To Die For* w. Laura Lippman," Janu-
     ary 19, 2022, in *You Are Good*, produced by Patreon, podcast, 40:01,
     https://podcasts.apple.com/us/podcast/to-die-for-w-laura-lippman
     /id1527948382?i=1000548362418.

27. Catherine Rottenberg, "How Neoliberalism Colonized Feminism—and
     What You Can Do About It," *The Conversation*, May 23, 2018, https://
     theconversation.com/how-neoliberalism-colonised-feminism-and-what
     -you-can-do-about-it-94856.

CHAPTER SEVEN: IT'S TIME WE TALK ABOUT NARCISSISM

1.   Kevin Donovan and Jesse Brown, "CBC Fires Jian Ghomeshi Over
     Sex Allegations," *Toronto Star*, October 26, 2014, https://www.thestar
     .com/news/canada/cbc-fires-jian-ghomeshi-over-sex-allegations/article
     _892cf877-a892-515b-b05f-7aa044c8eaa3.html; Manisha Krishnan,
     "CBC Court Motion Says Jian Ghomeshi's Lawsuit Is Out of Bounds,"
     Toronto Star, November 5, 2014, https://www.thestar.com/news/gta
     /cbc-court-motionsays-jian-ghomeshis-lawsuit-is-out-of-bounds/article
     _5c4fd362-44d5-54a1-b074-ad61c989527f.html.

2.   Alyshah Hasham, "CBC Fired Jian Ghomeshi After Seeing 'Graphic
     Evidence': Internal Memo," *Toronto Star*, October 31, 2014, https://
     www.thestar.com/news/gta/cbc-fired-jian-ghomeshi-after-seeing

-graphic-evidence-internal-memo/article_dfd15df0-6a0c-55bd-a5dd
-22be2b4eb9db.html.

3.   Author interview with Rachel Matlow, June 15, 2021.

4.   Ronan Farrow, "Episode 4: The Assistants," December 17, 2019, in *The Catch and Kill Podcast*, produced by Pineapple Street Studios, podcast, 10:43, https://podcasts.apple.com/dk/podcast/episode-4-the-assistants /id1487730212?i=1000459843067.

5.   Emily Grijalva, Daniel A. Newman, Louis Tay et al., "Gender Differences in Narcissism: A Meta-Analytic Review," *Psychological Bulletin* 141, no. 2 (2015): 261–310, https://doi.org/10.1037/a0038231; Tomas Chamorro-Premuzic, "Men Are Almost 40% More Likely to Be Narcissists. Science Explains Why They Often Become Leaders," *Fast Company*, March 4, 2019, https://www.fastcompany.com/90310927 /why-so-many-incompetent-men-become-leaders#.

6.   Paroma Mitra and Dimy Fluyau, "Narcissistic Personality Disorder," *StatPearls* (last update March 13, 2023), https://www.ncbi.nlm.nih .gov/books/NBK556001/.

7.   Julie Hall, *The Narcissist in Your Life* (New York: Lifelong, 2019), 24.

8.   Hall, *The Narcissist in Your Life*.

9.   Brian Resnick, "The Psychiatrist Who Wrote the Guide to Personality Disorders Says Diagnosing Trump Is Bullshit," *Vox*, February 17, 2017, https:// www.vox.com/policy-and-politics/2017/2/10/14551890/trump-mental -health-narcissistic-personality.

10. Rebecca Traister, "Abuse and Power: Andrew Cuomo's Governorship Has Been Defined by Cruelty That Disguised Chronic Mismanagement. Why Was That Celebrated for So Long?," *New York* magazine, March 12, 2021, https://nymag.com/intelligencer/article/andrew-cuomo -misconduct-allegations.html.

11. Traister, "Abuse and Power"; Mary Harris, "How New York Democrats Blew It," November 15, 2022, in *What Next* (*Slate* podcast), https://slate .com/podcasts/what-next/2022/11/did-new-york-democrats-midterms -cost-them-the-house-of-representatives.

12. Katie Nave, "I Can't Believe I Ever Called Myself 'Cuomosexual,'"

Elle, August 13, 2021, https://www.elle.com/life-love/a37294912
/andrew-cuomo-resignation-cuomosexual/.

13.   Tomas Chamorro-Premuzic, *Why Do So Many Incompetent Men Become
Leaders? (And How to Fix It)* (Brighton, MA: Harvard Business Review
Press, 2019), 4.

14.   Chamorro-Premuzic, *Why Do So Many*, 3.

15.   Chamorro-Premuzic, 54.

16.   Chamorro-Premuzic, 6.

17.   Jennifer Barnett, "I Left My Career in Prestige Media Because of the
Shitty Men in Charge and They Are Still in Charge and Still Fucking
Up," *Medium*, January 27, 2021, https://jenzerb.medium.com/i-left
-my-career-in-prestige-media-because-of-the-shitty-men-in-charge
-and-they-are-still-in-4963374ec6b8.

18.   Ijeoma Oluo, *Mediocre: The Dangerous Legacy of White Male America*
(New York: Seal Press 2020), 6–7.

19.   Oluo, *Mediocre*, 274.

20.   Christopher Lasch, *The Culture of Narcissism: American Life in an Age
of Diminishing Expectations* (New York: W. W. Norton, 1979), 59.

21.   Dennis Shen, "A Rise in Narcissism Could Be One of America's Political
and Economic Crises," *London School of Economics Phelan United States
Centre* (blog), https://blogs.lse.ac.uk/usappblog/2017/06/28/a-rise-in
-narcissism-a-root-of-americas-crisis/.

22.   Niraj Chokshi, "Attention Young People: This Narcissism Study Is All
About You," *New York Times*, May 15, 2019, https://www.nytimes
.com/2019/05/15/science/narcissism-teenagers.html.

23.   Jean M. Twenge and W. Keith Campbell, *The Narcissism Epidemic:
Living in the Age of Entitlement* (New York: Atria, 2010), 9.

24.   Twenge and Campbell, *The Narcissism Epidemic*, 68–69.

25.   Joshua B. Grubbs, Julie J. Exline, and Jean M. Twenge, "Psychological
Entitlement and Ambivalent Sexism: Understanding the Role of Entitlement in Predicting Two Forms of Sexism," *Sex Roles* 70, nos. 5–6 (2014):
209–20, https://doi.org/10.1007/s11199-014-0360-1; Sandeep Roy,
Craig S. Neumann, Daniel N. Jones et al., "Psychopathic Propensities

Contribute to Social Dominance Orientation and Right-Wing Authoritarianism in Predicting Prejudicial Attitudes in a Large European Sample," *Personality and Individual Differences* 168, no. 4 (January 2021): article 110355, https://doi.org/10.1016/j.paid.2020.110355.

26. Aline Vater, Steffen Moritz, and Stefan Roepke, "Does a Narcissism Epidemic Exist in Modern Western Societies? Comparing Narcissism and Self-Esteem in East and West Germany," *PLOS ONE* 13, no. 1 (January 24, 2018): e0188287, https://doi.org/10.1371/journal.pone.0188287.

27. Paul Verhaeghe, "Neoliberalism Has Brought Out the Worst in Us," *Guardian*, September 29, 2014, https://www.theguardian.com/commentisfree/2014/sep/29/neoliberalism-economic-system-ethics-personality-psychopathicsthic.

28. Gabor Maté (with Daniel Maté), *The Myth of Normal: Trauma, Illness, and Healing in a Toxic Culture* (New York: Penguin Random House, 2022), 31.

29. Lucy Mangan, "The Dangerous Rise of Andrew Tate Review—You'd Laugh if You Weren't Already Crying," *Guardian*, February 21, 2023, https://www.theguardian.com/tv-and-radio/2023/feb/21/the-dangerous-rise-of-andrew-tate-review-matt-shea-bbc-three.

30. Emma Bubola and Isabella Kwai, "'Brainwashing a Generation': British Schools Combat Andrew Tate's Views," *New York Times*, February 19, 2023, https://www.nytimes.com/2023/02/19/world/europe/andrew-tate-uk-teachers.html?searchResultPosition=1.

31. "Male Supremacy," Southern Poverty Law Center, 2022, https://www.splcenter.org/fighting-hate/extremist-files/ideology/male-supremacy.

32. Taylor Lorenz, "Incel Forum Pushes Rape, Mass Murder," *Washington Post*, September 22, 2022, https://www.washingtonpost.com/technology/2022/09/22/incels-rape-murder-study/.

33. Oliver Keenan and Agnieszka Golec de Zavala, "Collective Narcissism and Weakening of American Democracy," *Analyses of Social Issues and Public Policy* 21, no. 1 (December 2021): 237–58, https://doi.org/10.1111/asap.12274.

34. Agnieszka Golec de Zavala and Dorottya Lantos, "Collective Narcissism and Its Social Consequences: The Bad and the Ugly," *Current Directions in Psychological Science* 29, no. 3 (2020): 273–78, https://doi.org/10.1177/0963721420917703.

35. Dave McIntyre, "Sommelier Certification Has Become a Point of Contention," *Washington Post*, September 11, 2019, https://www.washingtonpost.com/lifestyle/food/sommelier-certification-has-become-a-point-of-contention/2014/09/11/d597f5ba-379c-11e4-bdfb-de4104544a37_story.html.

36. Author interview with Richard Betts, February 25, 2021.

CONCLUSION: CAN WE IMAGINE DIFFERENTLY?

1. Dafna Lemish and Colleen Russo Johnson, "The Landscape of Children's Television in the U.S. & Canada" (study commissioned by the International Central Institute for Youth and Educational Television), Center for Scholars & Storytellers, April 2019, https://static1.squarespace.com/static/5c0da585da02bc56793a0b31/t/5cb8ce1b15fcc0e19f3e16b9/1555615269351/The+Landscape+of+Children%27s+TV.pdf.

2. *Picture a Scientist*, directed by Sharon Shattuck and Ian Cheney (2020; PBS), DVD.

3. Yuval Harari, "Yuval Harari on His Advice to Young People for the Era of A.I.," ETFacetimeHome, July 17, 2023, YouTube video, 2:22, https://www.youtube.com/watch?v=5O77QN68u6U.

4. C. K. Lai, A. L. Skinner, E. Cooley et al., "Reducing Implicit Racial Preferences: II. Intervention Effectiveness Across Time," *Journal of Experimental Psychology* 145, no. 8 (2016): 1001–16, https://doi.org/10.1037/xge0000179.

5. "Indonesia's Matriarchal Minangkabau Offer an Alternative Social System," EurekAlert!, University of Pennsylvania, May 2, 2002, https://www.eurekalert.org/news-releases/837232.

6. Judy Mann, "Not a Question of Chromosomes," *Washington Post*, December 4, 1991, https://www.washingtonpost.com/archive

/local/1991/12/04/not-a-question-of-chromosomes/0f04a6f6-206d
-4139-a691-69e79ab2f199/.

7.   Shankar Vedantam, "What Does 'Sexual Coercion' Say About a Society?," *Morning Edition*, NPR, May 10, 2013, https://www.npr.org/2013
/05/10/182654664/what-does-sexual-coercion-say-about-a-society.

8.   Lila MacLellan, "Sweden's Gender-Neutral Preschools Produce Kids
Who Are More Likely to Succeed," *Quartz*, June 18, 2017, https://
qz.com/1006928/swedens-gender-neutral-preschools-produce-kids
-who-are-more-likely-to-succeed.

Index

male entitlement of, 185–86

narcissistic personality disorder,
    168–69

and neoliberalism, 182–83

normalization and growth of
    narcissism, 180–85

protecting the ego of, 173–74

racism of, 182

self-awareness of, 170

self-delusion of, 166–68

sexism of, 182

and toxic masculinity, 174–80

volatility of, 171–72

and white male supremacy, 179–80

women's vulnerability to, 167–68

narratives. See stories

Nave, Katie, 176–77

Nazis, 153–54

neoliberal agency, 119–20

neoliberalism

    and free will, 47–48

    and narcissists, 182–83

    neoliberal feminism, 162–63

    and personality, 183–84

    psychological impacts of, 48

    rise of, 48–49

    self-blame and shame promoted
        by, 49

    and trauma, 184

    on women's choices and
        empowerment, 137

    on women's sexual agency, 119–20

New America, 69

Newsweek, 117

New York magazine, 22, 144

New York Times, 21–22, 179

Nichol, Melanie, 158–59

Nisbett, Richard, 31–32

North Valley (Albuquerque), 121

Nyong'o, Lupita, 142

object constancy, 171–72

O'Donnell, Norah, 71

Oluo, Ijeoma, 179–80

Omega Institute for Holistic
    Studies, 79

orgasm gap, 139

Packnett, Brittany, 130

Paltrow, Gwyneth, 142

passion exploitation, 156–58

patriarchy

    as benefiting white women, 10–11

    calling out narratives of, 194

    as ghostlike forces, 8–9, 16

    imagining life outside of, 192–96

    and the impulse to shield the male
        ego, 72–73, 86, 173–74, 212n11

    and male entitlement, 9, 14,
        37–40, 79–80, 174–75

    via narratives, 8–9, 85, 194

    and victim blaming, 11–12 (see also
        victimhood and victim blaming)

    white women as foot soldiers of,
        125–34

women and girls (*cont.*)
  with the power to do anything,
    91–92, 95
  self-subjugation of, 124–25
  sexual objectification of, 90–91,
    95–97, 116, 138
  standards and cost of physical
    appearance and femininity,
    136–38
  stereotypes in English literature,
    86–87
  as wanting to be wanted, 132–33
  white, as threat to non-whites,
    125, 131–32
  white, individuality of, 127–28
Women's March (2017), 14
Wonderbra ad, 138
workism, 152–58, 164
workplace harassment and abuse
  dismissal of, 40–41
  increase in, 14

  and masculinity contest culture,
    149–50
  overwork, anxiety, and
    exhaustion, 146–51, 153
  passion exploitation, 156–58
  pride in enduring, 144–45
  romanticizing mistreatment,
    159–60
  by Rose (*see under* Rose,
    Charlie)
  toughness in the face of, 144–45,
    151–52, 158–64
World Values Survey, 42
Wynn, Steve, 33

Yarrow, Allison, 95
Young-Eisendrath, Polly, 132–33

Zakaria, Fareed, 67–68
Zeisler, Andi, 138
Zinone, Addie, 103–6, 108

About the Author

Reah Bravo is an American speechwriter currently living in Brussels. Earlier in her career, she worked in broadcast journalism producing political and other news segments for the PBS program *Charlie Rose*—a stint that ended in 2008, when she joined the untold number of sexually harassed women in America who leave their jobs. She holds a master's degree in international affairs from Columbia University and was a Fulbright Fellow in Bahrain.